W9-DFI-359

INDEX
ON CENSORSHIP

FRONT COVER: CONQUEST OF PERU BY PIZARRO FROM DE BRY 1590 (MANSELL COLLECTION)

BACK COVER: A 1941 PICTURE OF 'TAMIKO', A KOREAN COMVORT WOMAN WORKING AT A JAPANESE MILITARY BROTHEL

CAMERA PRESS

INDEX ON CENSORSHIP 3 1995

Volume 24 No 3 May/June 1995   Issue 164

Index on Censorship (ISSN 0306-4220) is published bimonthly by a non-profit-making company: Writers & Scholars International Ltd, Lancaster House, 33 Islington High Street, London N1 9LH
Tel: 0171-278 2313 Fax: 0171-278 1878
E-mail: indexoncenso@gn.apc.org
Internet Gopher site: gopher.iia.org:70
URL: http://www.bbcnc.org.uk/online/oneworld/partners/index/index_home.html

Index on Censorship is associated with Writers & Scholars Educational Trust, registered charity number 325003

Second class postage (US subscribers only) paid at Irvington, New Jersey. Postmaster: send US address changes to Index on Censorship c/o Virgin Mailing & Distribution, 10 Camptown Road, Irvington, NJ 07111

Subscriptions 1995 (6 issues p.a.): £32 (overseas £38 or US$48). Students £24/US$36

Former Editors: Michael Scammell (1972-81); Hugh Lunghi (1981-83); George Theiner (1983-88); Sally Laird (1988-89); Andrew Graham-Yooll (1989-93)

EDITORIAL

All change on the history train

'Historians are dangerous, and capable of turning everything topsy-turvy. They have to be watched,' said Krushchev in 1956 — one of the more candid admissions that people in power try to determine the history of their nations. It is a good moment to be looking at censorship in the writing of history. 1995 is a year of important anniversaries — of the end of the war in Europe, the liberation of the concentration camps, the first use of the atom bomb, the signing of the UN charter, the fall of Saigon — and of the first shot fired in the American War of Independence.

Some of the reordering of history has been particularly unsettling. In Germany a main thrust of the anniversaries this May has been to establish the sufferings of the German people rather than the horrors of Nazism. In Russia, key material from the Central Party archive has not yet been made available, despite promises. In Korea the story of the Korean 'comfort women' is only now being fully told — a story of 200,000 young girls kidnapped and coerced into brutal prostitution for the Japanese military, and brushed under the carpet for nearly 50 years by the Japanese, Korean and US governments. Now the women themselves have broken their silence. We publish one of their harrowing stories.

The comfort women exemplify what is so disturbing about revisionist history — that it is often a triumph of official orthodoxy, the voice of power obliterating the diverse voices of the people, for political ends. Even where the rewriting of history is a cause for rejoicing — the defeat of authoritarianism or racism, as in Russia or South Africa — there is still the danger of a new orthodoxy.

One safeguard against distortions of history is a free press, and we don't have much cause for rejoicing on that front. There are journalists in all continents who are under threat of imprisonment or death. On 3 May, World Press Freedom Day, Namassiwayam Ramalingum came into the offices of *Index* to report a *fatwa* on him in his native Mauritius for publishing a piece in his paper *L'Indépendant* which offended local Muslims (see p166). 'Our first step is to close the paper, then to kill Ramalingum.' Free speech, as ever, is a hard and costly business. ❑

Ursula Owen

CONTENTS

LETTER

Codes of silence

From Paulo Reis, editor-in-chief
Gazeta Macaense, **Macau**

I'm a Portuguese journalist working in Macau, a Chinese territory under Portuguese administration and due to revert to China in 1999. Political changes that have already taken place are threatening press freedom here.

In June 1994, a group of 17 local Portuguese journalists started to act against these threats, which, since 1991, have resulted in 24 complaints in court, and the condemnations of three newspaper editors for 'abuse of press freedom'.

Soon it will be my turn to go on trial (twice, as there are two different cases), also for the crime of abusing press freedom.

It should be noted that in the local judiciary system judges are chosen — and their terms are renewed — by a panel of seven members: the judge-president of the Macau Supreme Court (who presides over the panel), the attorney-general, two lawyers, two Chinese businessmen and a university law teacher. The formal appointment of judges is the responsibility of the Governor, who may accept or refuse the panel's decisions.

Just by curiosity, four of the seven above-mentioned members will be on the prosecution side, against me, in my first trial: the judge-president, Mr Farinhas Ribeiras, as plaintiff, and three other members as prosecution witnesses. These are not exactly the best conditions for a fair trial. And as the alleged victim of my 'crime' is a judge, the maximum sentence is two years in prison. The plaintiff in the second case is also the judge-president. Another curiosity is that, if I am found guilty and want to appeal, I will have to do so to the Supreme Court, where the plaintiff again is the judge-president.

The first case arises from a story about Mr Farinhas Ribeiras that I reprinted from the Lisbon weekly *Tal & Qual*. Mr Ribeiras also brought a complaint in Lisbon against *Tal & Qual*, but the Portuguese attorney-general referred the case to Macau. A local court, however, refused to accept the accusation of the Macau public prosecutor's office, saying that the court had no power to try a Lisbon paper. An appeal for clarification of this issue is currently pending in the Macau Supreme Court.

I'm sending you all this information and I ask for your help, as an organisation dedicated to defending journalists' rights and press freedom. Silence around what is happening in Macau is the main weapon which is being used against us.

The strategy to isolate me and argue that I am a lonely voice has been rather successful, I must say. Some of the most vociferous opponents of my opinions and positions are other journalists (with episodes including threats of physical violence coming from some of them).

To give you a practical example of this code of silence: between 7 and 10 April the Portuguese president visited Macau. None of the 30 or so journalists who came with him showed any interest at all in talking about problems of press freedom in Macau. Nor did any of the local journalists question the president about press freedom and human rights.

This happened less than a year after the president had said he 'was following closely the cases in court against journalists in Macau' and that he 'hoped the cases were handled with tolerance'; and two months after the US State Department's Annual Report on Human Rights devoted 11 pages to Macau, stressing the erosion of the independence of the judiciary owing to government influence, especially in cases against journalists.

A final detail: my lawyer on the first case (due to go to court on 9 May) told me on 12 April that he is giving up the case (he has been in charge of it since June 1994). I was notified by the court, on 21 April, that he submitted his resignation, as my lawyer, on 19 April. ❏

Gay legislation
Our listing of Gay Legislation (*Index* Jan/Feb 1995) should have recorded that all civil matters in Mauritius are governed by the Code Napoléon, and not by *sharia*. ❏

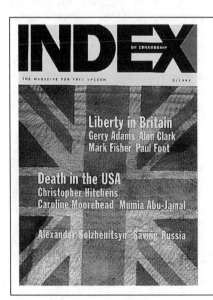

IN THE NEWS

NICHOLAS MCAULAY

Karachi kills me

A growing number of human rights reports highlight Pakistan's descent into uncontrollable civil violence

'Gangs and zealots tear Karachi apart.' 'Police arrest 160 after fresh violence.' Headlines like these, along with reports on the death sentence passed on a 14-year-old boy accused of blasphemy, the murder in broad daylight of 12-year-old Iqbal Masih, organiser of a union of child bonded labourers, and the recurrent outbreaks of sectarian violence, most recently highlighted in the murderous attacks on mosques, combine to suggest that Pakistan is disintegrating in a welter of uncontrollable violence and intolerance. The labyrinth of different sects, interest groups, political factions and regional rivalries is complex in the extreme, frequently impenetrable to the casual reader of news. Its roots stretch back to the creation of the country in 1947, the failure of democratic politics, recurrent periods of army rule, the unreconstructed feudal structure of society, and the bitterly divisive regional and tribal loyalties. Religion was not enough to bind the disparate units of this country, created when India gained independence from the British and Pakistan became the 'homeland for Muslims', the nation-state for which its founding father, Mohammed Ali Jinnah and the Muslim League had fought. The Mohajirs, Urdu-speaking Muslim migrants who fled India at the time of partition, were never integrated into the state and are today a disgruntled and angry community referred to still by 'true' Pakistanis — Punjabis, Sindhis, Baluchis and Pushtuns from the North West Frontier — as the 'refugees' (*mohajir*). The loss of East Pakistan, now Bangladesh, in 1971, put paid to the defining Muslim identity of the country and commentators prophesied its imminent breakup. The country has lurched from crisis to crisis, from civilian interludes to military dictatorships ever since. In 1995, civilian violence and sectarian tension are worse than they have ever been since 1947. A series of reports from international human rights organisations over recent months help to answer the questions: what is really happening in Pakistan? And why?

Thanks in large part to its political and bureaucratic elite, a powerful army and continued US support, a truncated Pakistan survived — at a price: after the brief civilian interlude under Zulfikar Ali Bhutto, government once again returned to the army and remained there for 11 years. The military regime of General Zia ul Haq that overthrew Bhutto in 1977 turned to Islam in pursuit of

JIM HOLMES/PANOS PICTURES

On the streets of Karachi: a swollen city sinking into violence

legitimacy and support, putting Pakistan in thrall to sectarian groups. The involvement of the USA — intensified after the Soviet invasion of Afghanistan — ensured the fracturing of the region along Cold War lines as it sought to balance India's ties with the Soviet Union. Military security agencies like the ISI (Inter-Services Intelligence) in Pakistan and the RAW (Research and Analysis Wing) in India developed a life of their own; the Punjabi-dominated army exploited the divisive political scene to rule the regions; and, from the 1980s, a new political force to be reckoned with emerged on the scene as the disgruntled Mohajir community organised for the first time into a coherent political movement.

The ethnic and sectarian rivalries that today dominate the violence that is destroying Karachi, Pakistan's largest city and capital of Sindh province, is popularly laid at the door of the Mohajir Qaumi Mahaz (MQM), a convenient scapegoat for a government with whom it is in bitter conflict and that has signally failed to control the mayhem on the streets of Karachi. Mohajirs are the largest single group in the city's swollen population of 11 million. The war in Afghanistan that drove two million Afghans to seek refuge in Pakistan added to the city's numbers and its reputation for violence. Karachi's Afghan community exploits its control of road transport by smuggling in supplies of weapons and heroin.

Altaf Hussain, founder of the MQM, claims that Mohajirs number 22 million in Sindh province, about 50 per cent of the population. Having quit India 'to build Pakistan', they consider themselves responsible for Karachi's economic success but remain outsiders to the feudal-regional power politics. Rather than accommodate or compromise with its demands for full political representation and, more recently, the creation of a separate Mohajir province, the government, aided and abetted by the army, has attempted to terrorise the MQM into silence.

The US State Department report, drawing largely on the work of the Human Rights Commission of Pak-

The monsters created by politicians and the army are out of control: the cost to Pakistan is incalculable

istan, is unequivocal in its condemnation of Benazir Bhutto's government. 'Although the Government made strong public commitments to address human rights concerns...most human rights abuses are rooted deeply in the social fabric. Government forces continued to use arbitrary arrest and detention, and have tortured prisoners and detainees. The government, as did previous ones, continued to harass political opponents and to repress the Sindh-based MQM.'

The section headings of Amnesty International's January 1995 report are sufficiently disturbing even without the harrowing details that elaborate their claims: 'Torture, including rape', 'Beatings, mutilation and sensory deprivation', 'Impunity of perpetrators'. At least 67 people died from torture during the first 15 months of Bhutto's administration and there were at least 35 extrajudicial executions. The torture of Zahid Ali Khan, a 25-year-old MQM activist, illustrates the ferocity used by the state against its political opponents. Arrested by police officers in the early hours of 22 June 1994, his family found his body later that day in a local hospital. 'His dead body showed his eyes gouged, his neck drilled, his ears chopped off, his shoulder and backbone broke.' Mohammad Murtaza, arrested with Zahid, says both had been hung upside-down for several hours during the interrogation session.

But it is not enough to recount the instances of brutality. The violence in Pakistan must be seen in the context of the three conflicts on its frontiers: the civil war in Afghanistan, the conflict in Kashmir and the troubles in Indian Punjab. Chris Smith's survey of the situation for London Defence Studies indicates that the arms used in ethnic and sectarian killings in Pakistan have their origin in the US-supplied weapons funnelled through the 'Afghan pipeline' via the Pakistan ISI and intended for the mujaheddin fighting the Soviet occupation of 1979-1989. Much of the weaponry found its way into the hands of the ISI — a former head of the ISI claims the organisation has stored three million Kalashnikovs — and, backed by money from the drugs trade in which the army is heavily involved, has since played a role in the region independent of governments. Smith claims the ISI has Islamist sympathies, conjuring a vista of terrorist networks supplied with ISI, US-supplied weaponry.

The role of the ISI has not been confined to lucrative deals in arms and drugs; it is heavily implicated in the deepening political turmoil. In an attempt to split Altaf Hussain's party it set up the Haqiqi (real) MQM. The result has been an inter-party feud costing many lives. Although evidence is limited, it is likely that the ISI also helped to train and arm the *taliban* who moved so swiftly and intriguingly into Afghanistan earlier

this year, and is involved in the civil war in Tajikistan.

The conflict in Indian Punjab has declined recently, but the fighting in Kashmir continues to escalate and is increasingly attracting international concern. The USA sees it as 'the most probable prospect of future use of weapons of mass destruction'.

The International Commission of Jurists report on human rights in Kashmir is more concerned with the legal situation in the disputed territory than in individual human rights violations. It concentrates on Indian Kashmir and the areas of Hunza, Gilgit and Baltistan in north Pakistan. However, there is an interesting chapter on Pakistan-held Azad (Free) Kashmir.

Azad Kashmir is home to over 30,000 refugees from Indian Jammu and Kashmir (J&K). The ICJ mission found their camps highly politicised, with movement back and forth across the ceasefire line into Indian-held territory. Of ISI activities in Kashmir, the ICJ says, somewhat tactfully: 'To the ICJ mission it was evident that the border between Azad Kashmir and J&K remains porous. Arms could also be channelled from Afghanistan into Jammu and Kashmir in this vicinity.' The Arms Project is blunt: 'Most of the weapons enter through the Haji Pir Pass and the Tosha Pass, the arc round the main road which leads from the border through Baramula to Srinagar...the ISI is the main body facilitating movement of weapons across the border to Kashmiri militants.'

As recorded by the US State

Department, the situation in Pakistan is unlikely to change. To check torture, murder and mass arrests by the state institutions would rock the boat too violently. Under pressure from the USA, Bhutto has made efforts to curb the activities of the ISI, but she too is part of the old social order and concerned to preserve her own power base. The collapse of the Soviet Union has opened up the vast resources of gold, silver, uranium, oil and gas in the newly independent republics of Central Asia to international exploitation in which Pakistan plans to play a leading role. It has already signed the Central Asian Transit Pact with China, Kazakhstan and Kyrgyzstan, and in March this year, was instrumental in setting up the Economic Co-operation Organisation, a trade and development union bringing together 300 million people in Turkey, Iran, Pakistan, Afghanistan and the six former Soviet republics, Azerbaijan, Kazakhstan, Kyrgyzstan, Tajikistan, Turkmenistan and Uzbekistan. One of the natural outlets for the region's produce is Karachi. The city's violence and endemic smuggling and corruption impede the investment urged by the government. The monsters created by politicians and the army are out of control: the cost to the impoverished population of Pakistan is incalculable. ❏

The Diffusion of Small Arms and Light Weapons in Pakistan and Northern India, Chris Smith (Centre for Defence Studies, 1993, 57pp)
Human Rights in Kashmir (International Commission of Jurists, Geneva, Switzerland, 1995, 140pp)
Pakistan — The Pattern Persists: Torture, Deaths in Custody, Extrajudicial Executions and 'Disappearances' under the PPP Government (Amnesty International, 1995, 55pp)
Afghanistan — The Human Rights Crisis and the Refugees (Amnesty International, 1995, 13pp)
Mohajir Nation a Victim of Gross Human Rights Violations in Pakistan (International Secretariat of MQM, 1995, 170pp)
India — Arms and Abuses in Indian Punjab and Kashmir (Human Rights Watch Arms Project, 1994, 59pp)
Human Rights Report 1994 (US State Department, 1995, p1245-1259)

RHYS JOHNSON

Silence in Gaza

Under pressure from Israel, the Palestinian Authority is coming down heavily on its own cities

'It was a hot heavy Gaza day. The heat of midday August on a bright spring morning. The stifling heat carried into the office. The staff were working without pleasure, without ease. I knew this would be the day they would come. I knew I would think about nothing else, none of the trivia of the day would distract me, it distracted no-one else either. In the afternoon, they arrived. Softly they came into the office but they cut through the atmosphere like a cold wind that seemed to spread from one staff member to another. Eventually, it reached me. I walked towards the room they were in. Looking at all the blank faces of the staff until I reached the door. They had only been there for a moment, but the air hung heavy with cigarette smoke. I closed the door...'

This rather Chandleresque opening, as well as hinting at my love of Philip Marlowe novels and my poor literary skills, makes a more serious point. There is a tendency among human rights groups to look for the dramatic gesture, the major violation of freedom of expression, the big news banning or closure, or even the death or injury of a person who had the courage to say too much. In reality, much of the activity of governments and societies is more covert, more sinister.

The story above is true. Its narrator is Raji Sourani, executive director of the Gaza Centre for Rights and Law, and a leading human rights activist in the Occupied Territories. On 1 April the Gaza Centre's board of directors came to the Centre and handed him a letter dismissing him from the post of executive director. This was the final act aimed at silencing the Gaza Centre.

The history behind the dismissal is linked to the Palestinian Authority. The Gaza Centre for Rights and Law had, from the advent of the Palestinian Authority in mid-1994, sought to maintain a positive dialogue with the Authority. But we refused to tolerate violations of human rights and regarded the State Security Courts, which President Arafat created in February 1995, as violating the rights to fair trial and liberty of the person. We strongly opposed the creation of the State Security Courts and actively sought their dissolution. The Palestinian Authority tried to silence the Gaza Centre's criticisms — by arresting Raji Sourani in February and by refusing permission for a legal seminar on these courts to be held. However, the Palestinian Authority did not succeed in silencing the Centre. Success came only when the board dismissed first Raji, then the staff.

The board have tried to convince the media that the dismissals were an administrative decision. But at the same time, the Palestinian Authority has referred to other factors; financial impropriety — 'they got a lot of money from the Ford Foundation', said the justice minister, Frieh Abu Medein. Attorney-general Khalid Qudra's comment was that it is illegal to 'cover your face and work politically under the name of human rights'. Here lies the problem in protecting freedom of expression; for a government, silencing critics can be as easy as cutting telephone wires, creating internal strife amongst staff or arranging for a board to dismiss employees from a critical organisation. No meetings are held, no public announcements made but the impact is the same. In some ways these tactics are more effective: they destabilise an organisation and undermine the confidence of its supporters.

This was the situation which faced Raji Sourani and his staff. It was only because of his international reputation and the events which led

JOHN TORDAI/CAMERA PRESS

Law in Gaza: Palestinian police take over

to his dismissal that links were made between the sackings and the Palestinian Authority.

We are now setting up a new human rights organisation, for which we need to register with the Palestinian Authority. To guarantee the registration we have remained silent about the Palestinian Authority's massive arrest campaign against political opponents and the trials of the State Security Courts which have denied defendants all the rights of fair trial. We hope that it will all be worth it.

In focusing on the problems facing us in Gaza, I have ignored the problems facing the Palestinian Authority. By any standards, these are huge. The Authority is beseiged on all sides, facing near revolt from Palestinians in the autonomous areas while Israel calls for ever more draconian measures to deal with this opposition. Nevertheless, it is a mistake to appease Israel by denying the human rights of the Palestinian people. Only with the safeguarding of these rights is peace a prospect. ❏

• On 27 April Amnesty International denounced the special military courts set up by the Palestinian Authority to quash armed opposition. Decisions reached by these courts are 'grossly unjust' says Amnesty, which is calling on the Authority to respect international agreements regarding fair trials.

LARA MARLOWE

No end in sight

Caught in the crossfire between a beleaguered government and the outlawed FIS, Algeria's journalists continue to die

After his killers stabbed him twice in the back, Smail Yefsah screamed repeatedly, plaintively, 'I didn't do anything. I didn't do anything.' It was eight o'clock in the morning and dozens of passers-by watched as three well-dressed young men then proceeded to shoot the young television presenter in the stomach and chest before making their get-away. Leaving a trail of blood behind him, Yefsah staggered up the stairs of his apartment building to collapse and die in a neighbour's flat on the second floor.

Smail Yefsah, murdered on 18 October 1993, was the seventh of 35 Algerian journalists assassinated over the past two years. The circumstances of every killing have been terrible. Many had their throats slashed or were shot at close range in front of their families. Yet because Yefsah's desperate plea of innocence — 'I didn't do anything' — summed up the feelings of a whole nation caught between security forces and Islamist guerrillas, his last words struck a chord in the minds of Algerians.

Some 40,000 Algerians have died in the rebellion that started when the country's first free parliamentary elections were cancelled by the army in January 1992. According to statistics released by security forces in March this year, 6,388 were killed in 1994. The figures provided by the government show that other professions have suffered greater losses than the press: 682 civil servants, 350 merchants, 304 peasants, 122 veterans of the war of independence and 101 teachers were murdered last year, compared to 21 journalists. But the latter represent a high proportion of the approximately 500 journalists still working in Algeria. And, as the ultimate form of censorship, the assassination of journalists symbolises the freedom of speech lost by all Algerians because of the war. The violence has severely stunted the young, inexperienced press corps which had begun to flourish after the 1989 Constitution was adopted. Until then, only official government media were allowed in Algeria.

The two best-known Algerian journalists to be assassinated, Tahar Djaout and Said Mekbel, wrote hauntingly prescient articles just before they were murdered. Djaout's last editorial in *Ruptures* [*Index* 4&5/1994] criticised the government for negotiating with 'backward' Islamists. Said Mekbel's daily column 'Mesmar J'ha' (Rusty Nail) in *Le Matin* bore the satirical nickname of former President Chadli Benjedid. Just about anyone who reads newspapers in Algeria turned first to Mekbel's witty, cynical, poignant missive each morning. His last piece was dated 3 December 1994, the day he was shot dead in an Algiers restaurant. In it, Mekbel described an

Algerian journalist as 'this thief who slinks along walls to go home at night...this father who tells his children not to talk about the wicked job he does...this man who makes a wish not to die with his throat slashed...' In homage to Mekbel, *Le Matin* has continued to reprint his columns.

For Algerian Islamists, there is no question of expression in the established, legal media. The clandestine fundamentalist radio and TV stations Wafa (The Pledge) and Inkad (Salvation) broadcast sporadically. Underground papers called *Raya Islamiya* (Islamic Banner) and *Ittissam* (Resolution) circulate in small numbers. To transmit a pro-Islamic Salvation Front (FIS) broadcast or print pro-FIS literature is to court death — in much the same way that journalists risk their lives going to work at the fortified ENTV headquarters on the hillside above Algiers or the well-guarded Maison de La Presse Tahar Djaout

Islamists denounce the 'selective indignation' shown by Algerian and western media that cover assassinations of well-known journalists and intellectuals but ignore the widespread torture and summary executions of fundamentalists by security forces. The Algerian media have observed almost to a fault the Orwellian guidelines handed down by interior minister Abderrahmane

The assassination of journalists symbolises the freedom of speech lost by all Algerians because of the war

Meziane-Cherif in June 1994: only the government version of violent incidents may be published, and then only on inside pages; Islamist successes are played down, atrocities committed by Islamist regimes in Iran, Sudan and Afghanistan are given wide coverage.

Islamists accuse government intelligence services of killing foreigners and journalists to discredit the outlawed FIS. In March, exiled FIS leaders formally condemned the killing of journalists and other non-combatants for the first time. But within days Rachida Hammadi, a well-known Algerian television journalist, and her sister Houria, a secretary at ENTV, were gunned down on their way to work. A week later, Mohamed Abderrahmani, publisher of the government newspaper *El Moudjahid* and the doyen of the Algiers press corps, met the same fate. So what of the FIS statement issued in Paris? Did it mean the leadership outside Algeria is cut off from the armed groups inside? Was the condemnation a public relations ploy by exiled Islamists fearful of losing their political refugee status in Germany and the US? Perhaps it meant only that the FIS political leadership is at odds with the more radical GIA concerning the assassination of journalists and other civilians.

I once asked the wife of an Islamist leader in Algiers how she could justify the killing of Djaout and others like him. 'An intellectual is someone who has taken sides,' she answered coldly. Sadly, secular Algerians who call themselves 'democrats' are equally categorical. When Abderrahmani was murdered on 27 March, an influential Algerian journalist understandably told me that while he didn't agree with Abderrahmani, 'no matter what a man writes, it doesn't justify killing him.' Yet earlier in March, the very same journalist had participated in a mock tribunal in which imprisoned FIS leaders were condemned to death. He apparently saw no contradiction between his campaign for press freedom and democracy in Algeria and the fact that since 1992 Algeria's Islamists have been deprived of all civil rights. ❏

NICOLE POPE

The cost of war

Turkey turns its back on Europe to go after its Kurds

Democratisation or isolationism? The question has never been more relevant in Turkey than it is this sunny spring. Since the beginning of March, the country's mood has swung from one option to the other.

March began with the signing of the customs union deal with Europe, a much-awaited event that sent a tide of euphoria across the country. Suddenly people saw the end of the tunnel. Everything was possible again, the democratic reforms seemed within reach.

But the rejoicing was short-lived. A week later, violent riots erupted in a poor neighbourhood of Istanbul, triggered by a provocative attack against the Alevi community, a minority liberal Shia Muslim faction that favours secularism. The target was well chosen to cause maximum disruption. The peaceful Alevi community, already on edge because of the rise of militant Sunni Islam and the tragic deaths of 37 of their intellectuals who were attacked and burned to death in a hotel in Sivas in 1993, rose to the bait and poured into the streets. Illegal extremist groups jumped onto the bandwagon and led protests that spread to other Turkish cities, fuelled by vicious police handling of the demonstrations. When the violent riots, displayed on western TV screens, abated after three days, at least 16 people had died — demonstrators say 30 — and hundreds had been wounded.

The incursion by the Turkish armed forces into northern Iraq proved even more damaging to Turkey's relations with its European allies. In the autumn of 1992, Ankara, co-operating with the Iraqi Kurds, had launched a similar offensive against the PKK bases in the north of Iraq, albeit on a smaller scale, and the West had said very little. This time, the reaction was almost immediate. Criticism and condemnations poured in from all over Europe, although the US government expressed a cautious 'under-standing' of Turkey's action. The Germans, the most outspoken, sus-pended arms shipments to Turkey, as human rights groups and internation-al organisations such as the UNHCR expressed concern both for the local Iraqi Kurdish population, and for about 13,000 Turkish Kurdish refugees who had fled the conflict zone in southeastern Anatolia last year to seek shelter in the protected safe haven north of the 36th parallel. Worse still, on 26 April the Council of Europe's Parliamentary Assembly voted a recommendation asking the Council of Ministers to suspend Turkey's membership if, by June, it had not withdrawn its forces from Iraq and improved its human rights situation. Turkey reacted angrily by pulling out of the Parliamentary Assembly.

The fact that so few foreign reporters were able to visit the area during the Turkish offensive fuelled accusations of wide-scale human rights allegations by the Turkish forces. As foreign correspondents kicked their heels in Diyarbakir, hampered by a rule introduced months before the latest offensive by the former foreign minister Mumtaz Soysal, allowing only journalists per-manently accredited in Turkey to cross the border, reports started filter-ing out of massacres of Kurdish shep-herds and numerous civilian victims of air attacks. On the whole, though, especially taking into account some of the actions by the security forces that have come to light over the years in southeastern Turkey, diplo-mats say the military seem to have been relatively careful in northern Iraq.

The success of the offensive, which is winding down — by 25 April, 23,000 of the 35,000 troops had been withdrawn — is, however, questionable. Despite official claims that 505 PKK rebels were killed, there was little evidence of fierce fighting among the 2,400-2,800 believed to be in the area at the onset of the campaign. The capture of large quantities of weapons and food may have somewhat slowed down the PKK, but, according to reports from the region, Kurdish militants began returning to the area only days after it was vacated by Turkish troops.

In Turkey, the offensive struck a nationalistic chord in the population: a fundraising campaign — 'Hand in hand with our lads' — successfully collected more than US$24 million for the armed forces. However, there were also questions raised about the wisdom of an operation — clearly the result of a decision by the mili-tary rather than by the government — that cost Turkey so much both financially and diplomatically.

The Iraqi adventure could have had a positive impact if the so-called success had been used to push through a reluctant parliament the democratic reforms that are much needed, especially if Turkey still hopes to make it to the increasingly unlikely October rendezvous with the European Parliament, which will have to vote on the customs union deal. Prime Minister Tansu Çiller promised President Bill Clinton these reforms would be adopted, including the lifting of the infamous article 8 of the Anti-Terror law, most commonly used against intellectuals and writers accused of 'separatist propaganda', which she herself described as 'shameful'.

Despite the fact that the population wants these reforms, the momentum seems to have been lost once again. Mrs Çiller has understood that constitutional and legal changes are a *sine qua non* for the implementation of the free-trade agreement with Europe, but she is facing strong opposition both from within her party — 30 of her deputies signed a petition against the lifting of article 8 — and from the opposition.

The debate still rages and some reforms may end up being accepted, possibly in a diluted form, but time is running out. In a few weeks, the Turkish national assembly is due to go into recess for the summer. If major progress has not been achieved by the end of June, it is a foregone conclusion that the customs union agreement with Europe will not come into force on 1 January 1996 as planned and a wonderful opportunity to anchor Turkey in the West will have been lost, or at least will have to be postponed. ❏

Iraq, May 1991: flight to a safe haven

ADEWALE MAJA-PEARCE

Suffer little children

Children as young as eight are recruited for battle by armed gangs fighting Liberia's civil war

I returned to Liberia after an absence of five years. The civil war which had begun shortly after my departure was still dragging itself out in large parts of the interior, but Monrovia, the capital, was under the control of a West African peace-keeping force.

I went first to my old hotel, but it was now occupied by squatters, refugees in their own country with nothing to do all day except sit on the balcony and watch the money-changers on Broad Street, or venture downstairs in search of food. I was later told that the Lebanese proprietor had fled back home just before Charles Taylor, the rebel 'warlord' who began it all, launched Operation Octopus in September 1992 in an attempt to dislodge the foreign troops and declare himself president. In the event, Taylor didn't make it, but the ensuing carnage, in which children as young as eight were recruited to join battle with trained soldiers (such was the scale of Taylor's desperate ambition), killed a quarter of the city's population. I was told a story concerning one of these children, a girl of 10 or thereabouts. Ironically, the story involved another Lebanese man by the name of Ghassan.

I had already heard about Ghassan from John, a tall, slight man in his mid-twenties who cleaned my room and fetched water and took me along to the basketball matches. It seems that Ghassan had once saved his life. It happened like this. One afternoon, during a lull in the fighting, John went out to look for food. On his way back, within sight of the building he and the others were occupying, he was accosted by a government soldier who asked him what tribe he was from, which was the standard question. John evidently gave the wrong answer. The soldier told him to strip to his underpants and follow him. 'By this time all the women were crying,' John said, whereupon Ghassan came forward and pleaded with the soldier, said that John was his son, and offered him 50 Liberian dollars (US$1) in one-dollar coins, which was all the money he had. 'If not for him,' John said and shook his head.

Everybody in Monrovia had their own story. There was AB, for instance, not yet 20, but already trying to build a small house for himself and his widowed mother on the plot he had acquired. I called him 'the philosopher' because he was forever trying to engage me in lectures (his word) about the meaning of life. He recounted to me on more than one occasion how his best friend was beheaded right in front of him. 'Did you know that a head does bounce like a football?' he kept repeating in renewed astonishment. He might well have wondered about the meaning of life; but it was another person, a young woman called Phoebe whose brother was trapped behind the lines, who told me about the 10-year-old girl soldier. It went like this.

One day Phoebe and Ghassan went out in search of food when a rebel jeep pulled up beside them. One of the rebels confronted Ghassan and said that he was going to kill him and drink his blood. Ghassan begged and begged but the rebel remained unmoved. Ghassan started crying as he entered the jeep, but as they were about to take off, Phoebe, even now not understanding what possessed her but knowing full well the possible consequences of what she was about to do, asked the rebel if she should come along also. He shrugged so she got in. Then she saw the girl in the front seat with an AK47 rifle across her lap.

They drove some distance from the city centre, the rebel all the while telling Ghassan that he was going to kill him and drink his blood. Finally, they came to a stop. The rebel told Ghassan to get down. Ghassan started pleading all over again and it was then that the girl made her move. She climbed out of the jeep as leisurely as you please, stood directly in front of the rebel, and calmly told him to leave the white man alone. The rebel refused. He insisted that he was going to kill the white man and drink his blood; that he had never before tasted the blood of a white

man. Suddenly, Phoebe said, the girl cocked her rifle, pointed it straight at his chest, and said that as his commanding officer she would shoot him if he didn't obey her immediately. Phoebe paused for a moment, searching for the words that would properly convey the meaning of what she had witnessed, and then shook her head. 'And he obeyed her,' was all she could add. The rebel stood to attention, saluted the girl, and got back in the jeep. Shortly afterwards, Ghassan followed his compatriots back to Beirut.

The 10-year-old girl soldier cocked her rifle, pointed it at his chest, and said she would shoot him if he didn't obey

Before I left Monrovia, I asked Phoebe if she had seen the girl since. She said that she hadn't, although she always looked out for her. The girl will be 13 now, if she's still alive; and I wondered at the bitter harvest for a country in which children had learned to kill or be killed: on 9 April, one month after I left, unidentified militiamen attacked the small town of Yosi in the interior, which is ostensibly under the control of Charles Taylor's National Patriotic Front of Liberia, and hacked to death 62 people. Although they were apparently armed with guns, the militiamen (or soldiers or rebels or bandits or whatever they call themselves) preferred to use machetes and clubs. Most of the victims were women and children, but then most of the victims usually are in wars of this kind. ❏

DARRIN WOOD

Net wars

Chiapas: the revolution will not be televised (but it will be on-line)

On 9 February President Ernesto Zedillo ordered the Mexican Army to move into territory held by the Zapatista National Liberation Army (EZLN) in the southern state of Chiapas. As Zedillo unilaterally broke the 13-month ceasefire between the two sides, his troops encountered a few stray dogs, some chickens and abandoned huts, but no ski-masked rebels.

Although the EZLN retreated into the jungles and mountains of Chiapas, along with thousands of their supporters from nearby villages, that doesn't mean they didn't fight back. They fought with the same weapons they have used since the truce of mid-January 1994: words.

The Zapatistas have been able to use words more effectively than most armies use tanks and artillery. Their communiques, signed by the enigmatic military leader Subcomandante Marcos (or 'Sup' as he calls himself), seem to be written by a literature professor rather than the revolutionary idol of the moment.

There are no long diatribes taken from Marx, Lenin, or Mao. Instead be prepared for citations from Cervantes, Garcia Lorca, Machado, or even the sonnets of Shakespeare — in the original English, with spelling and punctuation perfectly correct.

This has led some to speculate that Marcos is either hiding in a public library, or that he has a copy of the Complete Works tucked into his ammunition belt.

This is no ordinary guerrilla movement. There have been no executions. No assassinations of political leaders. No assassinations of the *caciques* (landowning elite) who control rural Chiapas, the traditional enemies of the indigenous Mayans who make up the Zapatista rank and file. They only 'fought' for 12 days, after which they called upon the civil society of Mexico, and the world, to finish their battle for them.

In the National Democratic Convention, held last year by the EZLN in territory under their control, they symbolically placed white banners on their rifles in the hope that one day all weapons would be silent. Since then, civil society, in Mexico and abroad, has done everything possible to make that dream a reality, using a weapon created by the US Defense Department over 20 years ago to do so: the so-called information highway of modem and internet.

Time magazine defined the new net-journalism in an article last year: 'Most journalism is top down, flowing from a handful of writers to the masses of readers. But on the Net, news is gathered from the bottom up — the many speaking to the many — and it bears the seeds of revolutionary change.'

Using new technologies for a third-world revolution is not entirely new. The Algerian revolutionary intellectual, Frantz Fanon, says in his book, *Studies in a Dying Colonialism*: 'Since 1956 the purchase of a radio in Algeria has meant, not the adoption of a modern technique for getting news, but the obtaining of access to the only means of entering into communication with the Revolution, of living with it. In the special case of the portable battery set, an improvised form of the standard receiver operating on current, the specialist in technical changes in underdeveloped countries might see a sign of a radical mutation. The Algerian gives the impression of finding short cuts and of achieving the most modern forms of new-communication without passing through the intermediary stages.'

The Zapatistas, and their supporters, have also passed through the intermediary stages as regards the possibilities of the modem. The latest communiques from the EZLN are posted on the numerous Mexican news bulletin boards and then downloaded and photocopied by groups in Spain to be handed out in demonstrations the following day. All of this cyberspace activism, or 'netwar', has caused concern in some sectors. Especially to Rand Corporation investigator David F Ronfeldt.

'The risk for Mexico is not an old-fashioned civil war or another social revolution... The risk is social netwar,' Ronfeldt has recently been quoted as saying, the fear being that traditionally factional opposition groups are more united in cyberspace than they ever could be in the real world. Mexican NGOs can stay in touch with sympathetic US or Canadian groups, and can orchestrate an international response to any government crackdown.

The effects of netwar aren't so far-fetched. Recent Internet postings requesting urgent medical attention for the EZLN's Comandante Ramona, currently extremely ill, were met by massive offers of help from around the world, within hours of being posted.

Long-time Mexican correspondent John Ross thinks Ronfeldt's comments are overstated, however. 'Anyone who has tried to get on-line through 'la neta' in DF [Mexico City] knows that the miracle of fibre optics isn't going to be the determining factor in the new Mexican revolution.' Ross sees the concern about netwar as just another attempt at censorship.

Several months ago, congressmen from the leftist opposition Party of Democratic Revolution (PRD) were claiming that the government had been interfering with their 'phone lines, the same 'phone lines that their modems were hooked up to. It should come as no surprise that new communications technologies are beginning to create new headaches for the world's censors.

Mexican actress and human rights activist Ofelia Medina said recently that 'the indigenous peoples are the intellectual avant-garde at the moment'. With their use of the modem and the information highways, it seems that they are becoming the technological avant garde as well. 'Zapata vive!' (Zapata lives!) is the current battlecry in Mexico. And Zapata is now on-line. ❏

Berlin 1945: East and West meet amid the ruins of victory

FELIPE FERNÁNDEZ-ARMESTO

Rewriting history

We live in an age of
iconoclasm: we have
felled Churchill,
Kennedy, Lenin, Mao.
Heroes come and go,
history marches on,
written and rewritten to
fit the needs of the time
and the exigencies of
political propaganda

In the film *Big*, Tom Hanks played a little boy who, trapped inside a grown man's body, had a brilliant career as a toy designer. One of his inventions was a computer that gave children the power to write and re-write their own versions of a story under a stock strip of vivid images. History has always been like the *Big* machine, clicking out colliding perceptions of the same events. It mutates according to a law of relativity: just as space and time shrink or expand relative to the speed of the observer, so our impression of the past seems to warp into different shapes according to the angle of approach. When I was a boy, my favourite book was *Pages Glorieuses de l'Armée Française* because it filled familiar wars with exciting battles of which the writers of my English and Spanish books seemed never to have heard. Within a single country or culture, the circumstances and needs of the time of writing become as much a part of the story as the episodes narrated and the people described.

Thanks to a healthy Pyrronist revival, this millennium is twitching to a close amid doubts about whether an objectively true version of the past even exists to be recovered: history, after all, happened to people who experienced it variously at the time, registered it mentally in contrasting patterns and recorded it in mutually contradictory ways. The onlooker is part of the event. Before historical writing disappears as a genre — to be reclassified by librarians alongside other forms of fiction — the approach of the year 2,000 creates a useful pretext for trying to track some of its trends. Although our way of counting time is conventional, dates divisible by 10 do, in practice, arrest attention and stimulate the imagination. The habit of thinking in terms of decades and centuries induces a self-fulfilling delusion and the way people behave — or, at least, perceive their behaviour — really does tend to change accordingly. Decades and centuries are like the clock-cases inside which the pendulum of history swings. Strictly speaking, a new millennium begins every day and every moment of every day. Yet both the Royal Albert Hall in London and the Rainbow Room on top of New York's Radio City were engaged for New Year's Eve, 1999, 25 years in advance. Most of the world's top hotels are already fully booked for the same evening and 'the Millenium [sic] Society of London and New York,' the *Daily Mail* reports, 'is planning a party at the Pyramids'.

A scramble to rewrite history in time for the party is already under way. Some kinds of historical revisionism are always with us. From time

Paris 1846: the glorious French army as street theatre

to time, a paradise gets mislaid or regained, as each period debunks the golden age myths of others and substitutes its own. Saddam Hussein presents his regime as a Babylonian revival; British fantasies, current or recent, are about a crime-free era when the unemployed got on their bikes. Particular groups tend to see their own past as a 'march of history' towards some goal — usually a complacent present — before discarding it when their complacency snaps. I call these stories 'sacred histories' because the obvious model is the Jews' struggle in a role assigned to them by Providence: uniquely among such myths, this Jewish reading of the past has never been discarded, unless the current secularisation of Judaism and the 'peace process' in the Middle East amount to its repudiation. Other, less durable examples are rapidly disappearing today: the Whig interpretation of English history (flowing unstoppably towards constitutionalism and democracy) still has a place in politicians' rhetoric but is getting weeded out of textbooks. The open skies over the 'Frontier Theory' — of an America fulfilling a 'manifest destiny' — have got clouded by a new multiculturalism which includes Blacks, Hispanics and Native Americans. Progress through class war to a classless society was seen finally to have lost its thrill when its objective was appropriated for one of John Major's slogans. And the historiography of the 'European Miracle', which spent a long time 'explaining' European superiority over the rest of the world, no longer seems to have anything credible to explain.

While sacred histories falter, classic 'turning-points' get twisted: events which at one moment seem to be of transcendent importance decline in significance from a perspective of lengthening time. Until recently, for instance, the Russian Revolution inspired cosmic language which now contrasts with the tendency to assume that its effects are already over. Other examples are the Industrial Revolution (the favoured term is now 'industrialisation'), the Reformation (now reclassified as a 'transition'), the fall of the Roman Empire ('the transformation of antiquity') and the Discovery of America (which, of course, never happened at all). We should expect nominations for important events of our own time to get downgraded accordingly: the rise of Japan, perhaps, the invention of the microchip, the Vietnam War, the demolition of the Berlin Wall, the forging of an 'ever closer' European Union, the Middle East peace accord, South African democracy....

Meanwhile, idols of previous generations are getting dethroned. We seem to live in an age of iconoclasm which has felled Churchill, Kennedy, Lenin, Mao; but heroes have always come and gone — selected and rejected according to criteria which change with the needs of the times and the exigencies of political propaganda. The few durable examples — Jesus, Muhammad, Alexander — survive because their attributes, like the outfits of an Action Man doll, can be swapped at will to match the peculiar values of any time and place. Alongside the fallen idols stand masked villains — bogeys of one period who get 're-appraised' at another. Villains get transformed by the alchemy of what C S Lewis called 'the historical point of view', which sees characters in the context (and according to the criteria) of their own time. Examiners now call this 'empathy' and it is an impassioning issue in the current educational debate in Britain. Reassessment can transmute the images not only of individuals — King John and Genghis Khan, Stalin and Hitler — but also of institutions and social practices. The Inquisition, human sacrifice, capital punishment, genocide — nothing is too bad to be justified by respectable appeals to moral and cultural relativism. One of the great dilemmas of liberal intellectuals in the new millennium will be to defend relativism while resisting its effects.

The biggest opportunities for rewriting history now are in the former Communist world, where topics have emerged from taboo and formerly proscribed versions are being rebuilt from the rubble. In a recent edition of the standard Hungarian historical atlas for schools, the 'Liberation of our Homeland' has been re-labelled 'Military Operations in Hungary, 1944-5'. In an accompanying volume for grown-up readers, postwar interventions in foreign countries by Russia, Cuba, Libya, Indonesia and India are illustrated alongside those of powers formerly classed as 'imperialist'. The Moravian Empire, the greatness of Lithuania in the late Middle Ages, the role of Free Polish forces in World War II are among subjects newly risen or restored to prominence in the historiography of their own countries. 'National' heroes are being re-elevated or invented: Genghis Khan in Mongolia, Alexander the Great in Macedonia, Gjerje Fishta in Albania, János Hunyadi in Hungary.

Decades and centuries are like the clock-cases inside which the pendulum of history swings

Meanwhile, the failure of political Marxism and economic Marxism has undermined historians' faith in historical Marxism. Despite agile writhings to deny it, Marx's predictions have proved false. The embitterment of bourgeoisie and proletariat has not happened as he supposed it would: instead the two classes have collaborated in mutual enrichment and, in the process, have become more like each other in manners, values, dress and taste. Some adepts of the old faith remain — indeed, their numbers are sure to recover after a while, as the disappointments of capitalism accumulate. At present, however, most students of the past are filtering Marxism out of their analyses. The eye-catching European political revolutions of the early modern period were once widely seen as the birth-pangs of a new society, struggling bloodstained from the womb of feudalism. Now they are being reallocated as little local difficulties. 'Class struggles' have disappeared from historians' discourse and even 'class' occurs ever less frequently.

The political changes which dethroned Communist regimes have also broken up big states, especially in Europe, where some peoples have recovered or are reasserting ancient identities. Some have attained devolution, autonomy or independence; others are calling or fighting for it. The agglutinative high-politics of Brussels, say, or Moscow, struggle with the amoeba-like micro-politics of the Caucasus or the Pyrenees. Disintegration is happening at the same time as integration. In consequence, instead of history written to legitimate empires and nation-states, we are now getting 'devolutionist' histories, addressed to a world of subsidiarity. When the policy of 'coffee all round' suddenly multiplied regional governments in Spain, cultural departments with budgets of their own invested heavily in identity-building projects for communities who sometimes had shallow historical roots. They became the patrons of scholarly monographs on regional subjects and of superb multi-volume histories of their areas of responsibility. Recent books on the history of European nation-states have reflected fissile experience, typified by Braudel's efforts in *L'Identité de la France* to do justice to the cultural environments of all those different kinds of cheese.

While we wait for the rest of the world to catch Europe's devolutionary virus, marginalised and minoritarian groups and regions

Point of arrival 1492: the natives discover Columbus.
From the Carta, *the first report of Columbus' voyage*

are getting the benefit of some of the historical attention formerly grabbed by metropolis, empire and state. The fashion for world history helps. World history, to me, is what happens at the edges, where cultures and civilisations, like tectonic plates, scrape against each other and set up seismic effects. Admittedly, the project of rehabilitating the overlooked seems sometimes to become just another way of piling up metropolitan history, because what gets recorded and transmitted is usually selected according to the centres' criteria of importance. The Hsiung-nu are known only from Chinese annals. We would know little about the Ranquele Indians were it not for Colonel Mansilla's interest in them. Children, women, the socially underprivileged, the sick, the 'mad' and the ethnic minorities have had to wait for elite perceptions to change before getting historians of their own. Yet work on recovering these 'lost' histories — with skill like a computer buff's retrieving long-deleted files — shows that history does have bigger potential even than the *Big* machine.

As well as by political change, historical revisionism is being stimulated by science. Historians, who formerly tried to crush the facts to fit Procrustean models and schemes, are beginning to enjoy the respectability of uncertainty. History is coming to be avowed as chaotic: a turbulence which happens at random or in which causes are often, in practice, impossible to trace; or a state of near-equilibrium, punctuated — like evolution, according to a current theory — by spasmodic change. It happens fast, like a snake darting between stones, tracked in glimpses and coiling unpredictably. After the long supremacy of gradualism, 'short-termism' — that vice of economic planners — has become a virtue of historians. Most of the long-term trends and long-term causes conventionally identified by our traditional histories turn out, on close examination, to be composed of brittle links or strung together by conjecture between the gaps.

The experience of changes — bewilderingly fast, barely predicted — in our own time has helped curtail the hunt for long-term trends: empires have vanished like snow in the river; industrialisation has leaped to unlikely places with the speed of a computer virus; and ideological fashions have emulated the readiness with which hem-lines rise and fall. Perhaps the most conspicuous trend of historiography in the last generation has been the squashing by revisionists of what were previously thought to be long drawn-out processes into ever shorter spells. The

English Civil War, for instance — long held by a faith compounded of partisanship and hindsight, to be the culmination of centuries of 'progress' — is now thought by most specialists to be best understood in the context of the two or three years immediately preceding its outbreak. The origins of the French Revolution and World War I have been chopped short by similar blades. Even what used to be called the Industrial Revolution is now seen as shuddering to a start, or series of starts, rather than accumulating smoothly.

Meanwhile, the relatively new discipline of historical ecology is breaking one of the oldest of historians' shibboleths. The first adjective has to be dropped from the motto, 'Homo sum et nihil humanum alienum puto.' The inclusion of Nature in the historian's world is an even more radical innovation than the incorporation of marginalised people. That human beings are only imperfectly studied apart from the eco-systems in which our lives are imbedded is a lesson taught to historians by political ecologists and by holistic trends in geography and anthropology. This is potentially revolutionary: though he occupies less of the picture, man is still the focus of historical ecologists' work but to the historian from Mars, perhaps, it will look as though wheat was the dominant species on our planet during our recorded history — cleverly exploiting human vectors for its propagation and global distribution.

Even as history succumbs to the influence of science, it is becoming less 'scientific' in the conventional sense. Out of structuralism and post-structuralism, a new humanism has evolved that relishes texts as evidence of themselves rather than as means to reconstruct events. A new antiquarianism has arisen, which ransacks middens and treasuries for instructive objects. Historians are getting out of the archives into the open air — walking in the woods, strolling in the streets, making inferences from landscapes and cityscapes. The avant-garde are incorporating oral research and personal experience into their work, to the dismay of those still trapped in the lanes of a race for objective truth. The best effect of these changes is that there are now again history books that are works of art as well as of scholarship. Great history, like great literature in other genres, is written along the fault-line where experience meets imagination. When well written, it has all the virtues of egghead fiction, plus better plots. Right now, the past has a great future. ❑

© Felipe Fernández-Armesto

EDUARDO GALEANO

A tale of ambiguities

Columbus died convinced he had been to Japan and the shores of China. And when it became clear that he had reached a land unknown to Europe, this gift of fortune was hailed as a 'discovery'.

Ever since, the indians have been, and still are, condemned for the crime of existing. Barely four years after Christopher Columbus set foot for the first time on the beaches of America, his brother, Bartolomé, began the burning of Haiti. Six indians, guilty of sacrilege, blazed on the pyre. The indians had committed sacrilege because they had buried small images of Jesus and the Virgin. But they had only buried them so that these new gods might make the corn harvest more abundant; they hadn't the slightest idea about sin or guilt.

Over the following centuries the black legend, just as much as the pink legend, multiplied the misunderstandings which marked America's entrance into western history. The two poles of this opposition — this false opposition — leave us outside true history, which has little or nothing to do with the history written by, and for, the victors. The black legend, just as much as the pink legend, leave us outside reality. Both interpretations of the conquest of America reveal a suspicious veneration for the past, that glowing corpse whose brightness dazzles and blinds us in the face of the present and daily life of our lands. The black legend loads the responsibility onto Spanish shoulders (and, to a lesser extent, onto Portuguese) for the immense colonial pillage, which in reality benefited other European countries in far greater measure, and which made the development of modern capitalism possible. Spain owned the cow, but ever since that far-off day when the Genoese bankers helped finance Columbus's first expedition, others took the milk. The notorious 'cruelty of the Spanish' never existed: what did exist, and does exist, is an abominable system which required, and still requires, cruel methods to impose itself and to grow. Correspondingly, the pink legend falsifies history, praises infamy, calls the most colossal despoilment in the history of the world 'evangelisation', and slanders God by proclaiming the new order in His name.

The black legend asks us to enter the Museum of the Good Savage, where we can shed tears over the obliterated happiness of a few wax figures that have nothing in common with the flesh-and-blood beings who people our lands. The pink legend, on the other hand, invites us into the Great Temple of the West where we can add our voices to the Universal Choir, intoning hymns in celebration of Europe's great civilising mission, to conquer the world in order to save it.

No to the black legend. No to the pink legend. To reclaim reality: that is the challenge. To change the reality that is, to reclaim the reality that was, the falsified, unseen, betrayed reality of the history of America.

In 1492, America was invaded, not discovered, in the same obvious way that in 218 BC Spain was invaded, not discovered, by the Roman legions. Furthermore, it should be said that America was not discovered in 1492 because those who invaded her would not, or could not, *see* her.

Of course Gonzalo Guerrero, the conquered *conquistador*, saw her and, for having seen her, died a violent death. Of course some prophets, such as the priests Bartolomé de Las Casas, Vasco de Quiroga and Bernardino de Sahagún, saw her and, for having seen her, loved her, and were condemned to solitude. But America was not seen by the many warriors, priests, notaries and merchants who came in search of a quick fortune, and who imposed their religion and their culture as sole and obligatory truths. Christianity, born among the oppressed people of an empire, had turned into the instrument of oppression in the hands of another empire that was marching into history with a seigneurial stride: the European empire of Charles V.

There weren't, nor could there be, other religions, only superstitions and idolatries; and any other culture was an expression of mere ignorance. God and Man inhabited Europe; while in the New World, demons and monkeys were dying. The so-called Day of Race instigated a cycle of racism from which all of America suffers to this day. Many are those who are still unaware that in 1537 the Pope decreed that indians were endowed with soul and spirit.

No imperial adventure — whether past or present— can discover anything. The adventure of usurping and pillaging does not discover

The hidden face of Peru: salvaging the old customs of freedom

anything: it covers up. It does not reveal: it hides. To realise its potential, it needs ideological alibis which transform the arbitrary into law.

The time has come for America to discover herself. This necessary discovery, the unmasking of the hidden face, presupposes salvaging some of our most ancient traditions. It is out of hope, and not nostalgia, that we have to reclaim the communal mode of production and life, founded on solidarity and not greed, on the identity relationship between mankind and nature and the old customs of freedom. I believe there is no better way of paying homage to the indians, the first Americans who, from the Arctic to Tierra del Fuego, have been able to survive successive campaigns of extermination and have kept their identity and their message alive. Today they continue to offer to the whole of America, and not only to our Latin America, the fundamental codes of memory and prophecy: they give testimony to the past and at the same time light the roadside lanterns.

I am not one of those who believe in tradition for tradition's sake: I believe in the spiritual inheritance that increases human freedom, and not in one that puts it behind bars. When I refer to the remote voices of the past that help us find an answer to the challenges of today, I am not suggesting reclaiming the sacrificial rites during which human hearts were offered up to the gods, nor am I praising the despotism of Inca and Aztec kings.

Rather I am celebrating the fact that America might draw, from her oldest sources, her youngest energies. The past tells us much about the future. If the values represented by real, living indians were of nothing but archaeological interest, the indians would not continue to be the object of bloody repression, nor would those in power be so intent on keeping them away from the class struggle and popular liberation movements. In our day and age, the conquest continues. The indians continue to atone for their sins of collectivity, liberty, along with other effronteries.

Their voices, past and present, always dangerous, still tell us that we are children of the land and that this mother is neither for sale nor for rent. As long as dead birds rain down on Mexico City and rivers are turned into sewers, seas into rubbish dumps, and forests into deserts, these obstinately living voices inform us of another possible world, which isn't one that poisons the water, the air, the soil, and the soul.

Their voices, past and present, also tell us of another possible world, which speaks to us of community.

The community, the communal mode of production and life, is the oldest tradition of the Americas, the most American of them all: it belongs to the ancient times and the first people, but it also belongs to the time to come and it promises a new New World. ❏

© Eduardo Galeano
Translated by Nathalie Vartanpour-Naalbandian and Martin Robinson

MARTIN WALKER

History wars

**Triumphant Republicans
fight to take control of
US history. Old myths
are reborn with terrible
consequences, newer
ones draped in dubious
glory**

Model cowboy: actors recreate the American myth

History is usually a battleground for its heirs. But the combination of historical anniversaries in the United States this spring has come with literally explosive force to a country whose political debates are being explicitly defined as a cultural war.

Three of this year's anniversaries were predictable, although their political effects have proved surprising. The date that nobody expected to commemorate was 19 April 1775, when the Minutemen of Massachusetts fired 'the shot heard round the world' against British troops at Lexington. The British planned to seize the militia armoury at Concord, and instead provoked a revolution which became a successful war of national liberation.

At that moment in Lexington, a recurrent theme of the American myth was born, as angry white men, hating taxes, opened fire to defend their right to bear arms. Two hundred and twenty years later, on the day hailed for its historical symbolism in the journals of the various new para-military militia movements, over 150 people died when a terrorist bomb exploded outside the federal building in Oklahoma City.

The first man charged in connection with the bombing was a former army gunner in the Gulf War who had been bitterly disappointed by his failure of the selection course to join the elite Special Forces. Timothy McVeigh, a gun-collecting militia enthusiast, wrote letters to his home town paper fretting over the plight of the US middle class, inveighing against gun control and the menace of overweening government, and suggesting that 'a new civil war' was nigh.

McVeigh represents an extreme form of a fundamental change that has taken place in the US political system over the past 30 years. The traditional politics of class, based on economic difference and benefiting the Democrats, have eroded. The new cultural politics benefit the Republicans. And they are rooted in racial politics and to specific wedge issues like gun control and abortion and the honour due to the US flag, all couched in the most militant of metaphors.

'America is facing a cultural war', Pat Buchanan, the candidate of the right, told the 1992 Republican presidential nominating convention at Houston. The ruins of the Los Angeles riots were still fresh when Buchanan summoned the party to a cultural Stalingrad: 'As the troopers of the 18th Cavalry took back Los Angeles, street by street and block by block, so we must take back our cities, take back our culture and take back our country.'

Today's themes of cultural politics relate precisely to conflicting versions of US history. 'Affirmative action' programmes, which give some modest advantage to racial minorities in jobs and education, were initially justified as a kind of belated justice for the suffering inflicted on blacks, Native Americans and Hispanics and even women in the past, and the hindrances that legacy imposes on them today. The new Republican determination to dismantle affirmative action as 'reverse racism' erases that historical sense of obligation.

The politics of the 1990s bring into anguished focus the other historical anniversaries that are forcing the US to reconsider its past this year. The fiftieth anniversary of the death of Franklin Roosevelt, who built the modern Democratic party as a vehicle of traditional class and economic politics, is the clearest reminder that an era has passed. And the twentieth anniversary of defeat in Vietnam, a war which saw the US working-class begin the great retreat from the Democratic party to the raw patriotics of the Republicans, signals the coming of the new politics of culture.

The fall of Saigon resonates so powerfully in the US today because it collides with the fiftieth anniversary of the US's proudest war, the one that established her primacy and her prosperity, the triumph over Germany and Japan in World War II. The good war, which had overwhelming national support and whose victory established the US's hegemony of the free world, confronts the bad and divisive war of Vietnam, in which defeat battered US self-confidence and soiled its moral authority.

'America is facing a cultural war. We must take back our cities, take back our culture, take back our country'.

Pat Buchanan, Republican presidential candidate 1992

There are powerful historic currents swirling here. Republicans and Democrats alike try to claim FDR as an inspirational icon, just as the concept of the big and caring federal government which Roosevelt crafted is being dismantled by a Republican Congress, whose political dominance reflects the final passing of the old Roosevelt political coalition. The Roosevelt voting coalition of industrial workers and trade unions, poor whites of the south and urban blacks, liberals and intellectuals, was the basis of the Democratic Party's era of dominance until civil rights began to peel off the south.

The only US president to be re-elected three times, Roosevelt long after death retained his extraordinary dominance of the US political system. His New Deal of Keynesian economics and social security endured as the guiding principles of US government for a generation. And now, finally, it is over. The domestic legacy of Franklin Roosevelt has lasted exactly 50 years. The success of the new generation of Republicans in Congress in passing their 'Contract with America' signals the final crisis of the era of big government which Roosevelt's New Deal

CAMERA PRESS

Slave auction, Virginia: history creates a sense of obligation, now denied

launched to combat the Great Depression.

It is in contemporary presidential politics that one can most clearly see these historical chickens coming home to roost. In the 1992 presidential election campaign, the first of the baby-boomers beat the last of the grandfathers as Clinton defeated George Bush. Now that reliable old generation rides once more, as Republican Senate leader Bob Dole, last of the World War II heroes, challenges the baby-boomer who ducked the Vietnam war. The extraordinary potency of this Vietnam anniversary has been sharpened by the publication of the anguished memoirs of President Kennedy's and President Johnson's secretary of defence, Robert McNamara.

It can be summed up in one implacable sentence — 'We were wrong, terribly wrong.' McNamara's central apologia bears quotation at some length. 'I truly believe that we made an error not of values and intentions but of judgement and of capabilities... We failed to ask the five most basic questions: was it true that the fall of South Vietnam would trigger the fall of all South East Asia? Would that constitute a grave threat to the West's security? What kind of war — conventional or guerrilla — might develop. Could we win it with US troops fighting alongside the South Vietnamese? Should we not know the answers to all these questions before deciding whether to commit troops?

'It seems beyond understanding, incredible, that we did not force ourselves to confront such issues head-on. But then, it is very hard, today, to recapture the innocence and confidence with which we approached Vietnam in the early days of the Kennedy administration. We knew very little about the region.'

McNamara has been bitterly criticised by both sides of the argument as the hawks and doves of that gruesome era once more beat their wings over the US airwaves. The passions are as strong as ever. The anti-war case was most pungently put by a grimly sanctimonious *New York Times* editorial which said: 'Mr McNamara must not escape the lasting moral condemnation of his countrymen...his regret cannot be huge enough to balance the books for our dead soldiers.'

From the other side, William F Buckley, the high priest of US conservatism for 40 years, reviewed McNamara's book as yet another exhibit in a pitiful lack of national moral fibre. 'South Vietnamese power, backed by the US military, very nearly toppled the Communist revolution; if the Christmas bombing in 1972 had been followed by a modestly manned invasion of Hanoi by the South Vietnamese, backed by the US military, Ho's heirs would have had to fly the coop and mend their sores in Peking'.

The US's TV screens and magazines, the vehicle and triggers of the popular memory, were this April and May jumbling together the images of the wrecked building of Oklahoma City with the wreckage of 1945 Berlin. And interrupting them came eerily familiar scenes. A helicopter in silhouette, leaking a hapless trail of people across a desolate rooftop, all etched against a hauntingly grey tropic sky. A Soviet-made tank, nosing insolently through the gates of the presidential palace in Saigon.

Twenty years on, what lingers are the images of that unique event, a US defeat. Every other US military setback, from Custer's Last Stand to the Japanese attack on Pearl Harbor, has later taken its place as another tragic but heroic milepost on the road to eventual victory. That is how nations construct their sustaining myths, draping the bitterness of defeat in the triumphal garments of eventual victory.

And that is how the USA over the past 20 years has slowly sought to devise an acceptable historical context for its humiliation in Vietnam, as one lost battle in the long but ultimately victorious war against Communism.

'You take the long historical view, and you'd have to say that whatever happened in the past, the Vietnamese people are now turning to American values and American free enterprise and democracy, which is what we were fighting for,' says Senator John McCain of Arizona.

A navy pilot who was shot down and became a prisoner of war in Hanoi, McCain later entered politics and is now a conservative US senator for the Republican party. His election pamphlets depict his happy return, limping in his Navy whites to the homecoming after years of imprisonment.

McCain's claim of a delayed victory is a common view among the military men. And it goes with another myth, of American warriors stabbed in the back. In the words of General William Westmorland, the commander in Vietnam during the military build-up: 'We were winning that war on the battlefield, and in the hearts and minds of the South Vietnamese people who sought our help against the march of Communism, until we lost it in Washington, on the TV screens and in the newspapers and on college campuses.'

Vietnam's own *perestroika* and its return to the free market and its wooing of western businessmen have helped reassure US citizens that they were on the right side of history all along. It is a comforting conclusion, fit for Hollywood in its assumption that Vietnam had its own happy ending and in its refusal to acknowledge US responsibility for the decades of horror that were inflicted on South East Asia.

Until McNamara's book appeared, the country had come to an uneasy accommodation with its memories of the war. Hollywood helped exonerate the troops. The Gulf War helped to rehabilitate the military as high-tech wonderboys who could deliver US victories without US casualties. And now, as Roosevelt's political legacy crumbles before the Republican revisionists, the Gulf War delivers Timothy McVeigh to bring home not just the extreme edge of the cultural war, but the explosives and the casualties of war itself. ❏

RONALD DWORKIN

The unbearable cost of liberty

Denying the Holocaust is a monstrous insult to the memory of the Jews and others who perished in it. But Germany solves nothing by making it a criminal offence

Over the past year an important free-speech drama has been unfolding in Germany. In 1991, Guenter Deckert, leader of the ultra-right-wing National Democratic Party, organised a meeting at which Fred Leuchter (a US 'expert' who has designed gas chambers for US prisons) presented his 'research' purporting to show that the Auschwitz gassing of Jews never took place. Though Leuchter's arguments were already well publicised around the world, Deckert was prosecuted and convicted for arranging the lecture under a statute prohibiting incitement to racial hatred. In March 1994, the Federal Court of Justice overturned the conviction on the ground that just denying the Holocaust does not automatically constitute incitement, and it ordered a new trial to determine whether the defendant 'sympathised with Nazi beliefs' and was guilty of 'insulting and denigrating the dead'.

Deckert was tried and convicted again: three trial court judges said he did sympathise with Nazi beliefs and did insult the dead. But they gave him only a suspended one-year jail sentence and a light fine, declaring that his only crime consisted in expressing an opinion, and adding, incredibly, that he was a good family man, that his opinions were from 'the heart', and that he was only trying to strengthen German resistance to Jewish demands. Two of the judges were soon relieved of their duties for 'long-term illness', the only available ground for that action, and though they have quietly returned to their court they continue to be criticised by other judges, some of whom refuse to sit with them. Last December, the Federal Court of Justice overturned Deckert's light sentence, and ordered yet another trial.

The public was outraged by the series of events, and the law responded. In April 1994, the German constitutional court declared that denials of the Holocaust are not protected by free speech, and upheld an official ban on a right-wing conference where the controversial British historian of the Holocaust, David Irving, was to present his views. Early this year the German Parliament passed a new law declaring it a crime, punishable by five years in prison, to deny the Holocaust, whether or not the speaker believes the denial.

The new law has been vigorously enforced: in March, German police

CAMERA PRESS

Wartime Prague: hostage to evil

searched the headquarters of a far-right newspaper and seized copies of an issue reviewing a Danish Holocaust-denying book. The law has also produced problems of interpretation. In February, a Hamburg court decided that someone who left a message on an institutional answering machine stating that Steven Spielberg's *Schindler's List* won an Academy Award because it perpetuated the 'Auschwitz myth' was not guilty of the crime. That decision, which generated a new furore, is now on appeal, but if it is reversed neo-Nazis will undoubtedly test the law with a variety of other locutions until they find one that is sustained and can become a new code phrase. They are, of course, delighted with trials turning on speech, because these provide brilliant forums for their views — the Munich trial of Ewald Althans, another Holocaust denier, featured hours of videos of Hitler's speeches and other neo-Nazi propaganda.

The German Constitution guarantees freedom of speech. What justifies this exception? It is implausible that allowing fanatics to deny the Holocaust would substantially increase the risk of fascist violence in Germany. Savage anti-Semitic crimes are indeed committed there, along with equally savage crimes against immigrants, and right-wing groups are undoubtedly responsible for much of this.

> Anyone who interprets National Socialism as merely a political movement knows almost nothing about it. It is more than a religion. It is the determination to create the new man
>
> *Hitler*

But these groups do not need to deny that Hitler slaughtered Jews in order to encourage Hitler worshippers to attack Jews themselves. Neo-Nazis have found hundreds of lies and distortions with which to inflame Germans who are angry, resentful and prejudiced. Why should this one be picked out for special censorship, and punished so severely?

The real answer is clear enough: it was made explicit in the reactions of Jewish leaders to the legal events I have described, and in the constitutional court's opinion. Denying that the Holocaust ever existed is a monstrous insult to the memory of all the Jews and others who perished in it. That is plainly right: it would be ghastly, not just for Jews but for Germany and for humanity, if the cynical 'Auschwitz lie' were ever to gain credibility. It should be refuted publicly, thoroughly and contemptuously whenever it appears.

But censorship is different. We must not endorse the principle that opinion may be banned when those in power are persuaded that it is false and that some group would be deeply and understandably wounded by its publication. The Creationists who banned Darwin from the Tennessee public schools in the 1920s were just as convinced about biological history as we are about German history, and they, too, acted to protect people who felt humiliated at the centre of their being by the disgraceful new teaching. The Muslim fundamentalists who banned Salman Rushdie were convinced that he was wrong, and they, too, acted to protect people who had suffered deeply from what they took to be outrageous insult. Every blasphemy law, every book-burning, every witch-hunt of the right or left, has been defended on the same ground: that it protects fundamental values from desecration.

Beware principles you can trust only in the hands of people who think as you do. It is tempting to say that Germany's situation is special, that the Holocaust was off history's graph and calls for exceptions to everything, including freedom of speech. But many other groups believe their situation special too, and some have good reason. There is nothing like the Holocaust in US history, but slavery is bad enough. Blacks find arguments like those of Herrnstein and Murray's book, *The Bell Curve*, which suggests that races differ genetically in intelligence, deeply offensive, and in some US universities, professors who teach a view of history that minorities believe insulting are ostracised and disciplined. We would not want people in power, who thought this biology or history plainly wrong, to have the right to ban it. Censorship is often the child of grievance, and people who feel that history has been unjust to them — as many Muslim fundamentalists and other groups as well as blacks do — are unlikely to accept that their position is not special too.

I know how strong the case for censorship seems in Germany now; I know that decent people are impatient with abstract principles when they see hoodlums with pseudo-swastikas pretending that the most monumental, cold-blooded genocide ever was the invention of its victims. The hoodlums remind us of what we often forget: the high, sometimes nearly unbearable, cost of freedom. But freedom is important enough even for sacrifices that really hurt. People who love it should give no hostage to its enemies, like Deckert and his odious colleagues, even in the face of the violent provocations they design to tempt us. ❏

BARUCH KIMMERLING

Shaking the foundations

Independence Day 1948: first day of the State of Israel

The Middle East peace process has thrown up some interesting side-effects within Israel, one of which, fuelled by the recent opening of the state archives for 1935-1955, is an unprecedented re-examination of its history, in particular the period immediately before and after the founding of the state in 1948. The great history debate, remorselessly aired in the media, has divided generations and driven the old guard to a bitter defence of their turf against the encroachments of the 'new historians'. Benefiting from hitherto secret documents, the latter accuse the academic establishment and the Israeli ministry of education of developing an 'official' version of Jewish history in which the facts are sacrificed to 'self-justifying' myths. Many in the older generation of academics, themselves responsible for the founding myths, accuse the new historians of destroying the foundations of the state and threatening its legitimacy. On the contrary, their opponents argue, it is precisely because Israel has come of age, is strong and its right to exist now recognised by former enemies, that a new, non-ideological history can be born

Aaron Meged, (born in 1920 and one of the foremost Israeli novelists in the early days of the state) accuses an assorted group of historians and researchers whom he labels collectively the 'new historians' of rewriting the history of Zionism in the image of its enemies: of dedicating themselves to the destruction of Zionism by sapping its legitimacy. He detects a 'suicidal instinct' in Israeli society and is amazed at its propensity to hasten its own demise.

Meged's article exploits the current malaise in our society that is born of peace-phobia. For a long time now, we have learned to live with a perpetual state of war. The prospect of change plunges Israeli Jews into a state of anxiety and panic. We have always claimed we wanted peace, but have imagined it as some remote, doomsday phenomenon. Now that peace actually threatens to break out, Israelis are faced with a situation they have no idea how to handle. Those who are afraid immediately look for scapegoats and traitors.

Ideological mobilisation within Israel has always presented human scientists and historians with a problem: professional ethics demand complete objectivity and a strict regard for the facts free of political considerations or regard for 'official' versions of events. Faced with the competing demands of their profession and the requirements of the state, many gave up the unequal struggle.

The founding fathers of Israeli social sciences were faced with a paradox. One aspect of the Zionist vision demanded that they create a quality science free of ideological bias. But Zionism also needed 'committed' scholarship. Caught in this double bind, their record is mixed: the scholarly legacy of history and the social sciences in the universities is an honourable one; but we cannot be said to have done our utmost to achieve ideological independence.

The heart of the matter

The history debate rages most passionately round discussion of the Shoah. Tom Segev — who does not identify with the 'new historians' — raises it in his book The Seventh Million *(1994). Debate centres on the politics of Zionism and its humanitarian role. In 1938, Ben Gurion said: 'Better save only a proportion of the German children for fear all will descend on Eretz Israel'. Today people ask if the leaders of the Zionist movement before 1939 put Jewish immigration into Israel above the need to save German Jewry? Did Ben Gurion, after 1942, willingly sacrifice humanitarian action to good relations with the Allies, in particular Roosevelt? Immediately after the war, the Zionist right and extreme right accused the leaders of the Labour Party of complying with the US refusal to intervene against the 'final solution', thereby preventing them from mobilising Jews in the USA.*

Israel developed a form of scholarship — at least in everything that touched on Jewish-Zionist concerns — committed to the ruling interests, those of the socialist workers' movement, chiefly the Labour Party. It was an Ashkenazi view and, to a degree, chauvinist. Every Middle East historian at the time — and others too — knew how the Arabs of Palestine/Eretz Israel had been driven into exile and how and why they were prevented from returning. Benny Morris, an historian in the classic mould and a compulsive digger in the archives, whose *Origins of the Palestinian Refugee Problem from 1947-1949* created such a scandal when it was published in Israel in 1991, demonstrates that while there was no premeditated plan for their mass expulsion, in the event, no-one attempted to stop the flight of the Palestinians and that the Jews were, indeed, responsible for their expulsion. Chaim Weizmann, first president of Israel, said privately that the 'real miracle' of 1948 was not the Jews' military success, but the 'cleansing of the country' of a considerable part of its Arab population. But Israeli historiography has imposed a taboo on this subject. The failure to ask certain questions is, and remains, one of the hallmarks of 'committed' scholarship.

Morris failed to play by the rules of the academic establishment and was stigmatised as a 'revisionist' in the same negationist category as, for instance, Robert Faurisson who denies the Shoah.

Despite the taboos, however, the Arab problem has not always been

The refugee question

The official version of the Palestinian refugee question taught in Israeli schools has it that the 1948 flight of Palestinians was a voluntary response to a call from the mufti of Jerusalem. In his Origins of the Palestinian Refugee Question, *Benny Morris demonstrates that the facts tell a different tale. A minority certainly fled to join the Arab armies; the vast majority of civilians simply fled before an advancing army and the collapse of their own institutions; an even smaller minority were terrorised or driven out at gunpoint.*

Supported by the archives, Morris confirms the existence of 'Programme D'. From 1947-1949, this authorised the military to 'cleanse the conquered territories, including the expulsion of the entire population of Arab villages', as, for instance, in the townships of Lod and Ramallah.

In Arab Israelis, Sub-Tenants, *Uzi Benziman and Ataullah Mansour, write: 'Even after the ceasefire of 1949, there were massive expulsions, the most infamous of which was that of the entire population of Majdal, today Ashkelon, in 1950.' They comment: 'Even if the idea of "transferring" the Palestinian population only played a limited role in events, it testifies to a certain mentality: get rid of the Arabs.'*

forbidden ground. The taboo came to the forefront and remained there in the time immediately preceding and after the creation of the Jewish state when it was a question of deciding what relationship should be established between Jews and Arabs. The problem was that Israeli social scientists had, for many years, envisaged Israeli society without Arabs; sealed off from the impact of war and conflict.

Meged is asking for a return to committed scholarship. He also, quite explicitly, demands a return to the myths: he wants 'Zionist scholarship', ideological scholarship, non-scholarship. Anything other than this endangers 'our legitimate rights', hence his pseudo-Freudian theory around a supposed 'Israeli suicide wish'. He also alleges that some Israeli intellectuals have been mobilised to bring about the most cherished desire of the Arabs — the destruction of the State of Israel — through their anti-Zionist history.

Meged drags up the old accusation against academics who claim that a form of colonialism was implicit in Zionism from its origins and not from the conquest of the West Bank in 1967. The 'proofs' he cites to counter this, guaranteed to get Israeli backs up, do not stand up to the facts.

Israeli academics always adopt a comparative approach in their study of other societies. Were the same method applied to the study of Israeli society, the same type of immigrant/colonial society as in North and South America, Australia, South Africa and Algeria would emerge.

None of which belittles the 2,000-year-old longing of Jews for Zion. This, too, is an established cultural and political fact and must be integrated into our 'History'. But it does not change the facts of the 'colonial situation' in which people from different parts of the world gathered in a particular place and built their society and state on the ruins of another. They failed to crush its inhabitants who, in turn, failed to repulse them. A classic colonial scenario.

'The people who live in Zion' have become strong enough and sufficiently well rooted to confront their own origins and history. Historians and social scientists who are expected to provide 'the people' with a neatly packaged history, invented, distorted and, above all, based on the kind of myths that Meged so ardently desires, are abusing their role as scholars as well as their social and intellectual duty.

Such attitudes provide powerful ammunition for the escalating efforts

Military necessity

Between 1951 and 1956, the Israeli army conducted a series of punitive operations against Palestinian villages in Gaza and Jordan. Officially, their purpose was to persuade King Hussein and Gamal Abdul Nasser to disarm the Arab fighters (fedayin). One such raid was on the village of Kybia where around 50 civilians were killed in cold blood on the night of 12 October 1953. Prime Minister Ben Gurion claimed this was a matter of private vengeance by a group of Israelis outraged by an attack. However, the archives published by Benny Morris show this was entirely a military affair, sanctioned and supervised in person by Ben Gurion to terrorise the Palestinian population.

For most Israelis, the story touches the heart of the current debate. It calls into question a fundamental precept taught to every schoolchild: that Israel fought only in self-defence and therefore kept its military 'pure'.

of a well entrenched group of elderly academics to discredit the work of researchers who are not part of the Israeli academic establishment, most of whom are young and vulnerable. Seeing themselves defeated on their own ground, the historical mandarins are turning to the media to mobilise public opinion against the 'traitors' by manipulating the fear and apprehension through which the country is now going. They feel the earth trembling beneath their feet, their teaching no longer up to the challenge presented by the upheavals taking place in Israeli historiography — a regular phenomenon in western scholarly circles. If they are to protect their preserve, they have no other choice than to declare war on Israeli scholarship and the wider academic world.

If the new historians are now examining the problem of legitimacy or 'the right of Jews to this land', it is not in order to confirm or deny this 'right': the social sciences are not concerned with morals. The questions are posed to analyse the effect on society and to explore how this can best be handled. Something that will continue to exercise our scholars and historians, as well as our writers in unpredictable ways. ❏

Originally published in Ha'Aretz. *Translated from the French by Judith Vidal-Hall*

David Ben Gurion: founding father and myth maker

ROBERT SERVICE

What future for the Russian past?

Historical research and publication are freer now than at any time in Russia's past. History is no longer seen through the single vision of the great leader, but has fragmented into a kaleidoscope of views that put the people back into the picture

History in Russia has always been beset by political problems of the most overt kind. All writers were constrained to glorify Lenin, the October Revolution, the Communist Party and the traditions, institutions and policies of the USSR. By forcing textbooks on to this line, the Politburo aspired to convince its society that the Soviet order had been the legitimate expression of popular aspirations since 1917.

In 1991 the Soviet order disintegrated; the state itself ceased to exist. Boris Yeltsin announced the end to a 'totalitarian regime with radical policies of reform'. And these policies included a rupture with the last remaining controls over research and publication on the Soviet past.

A new epoch in scholarly and popular historical writing was heralded; and in many way there were grounds for optimism. The old Central Party Archive was opened to Russian and foreign historians; articles in the press indicated an increasing willingness to print the previously unprintable; debates among scholars on TV prepared society to reconsider all the once hallowed verities of 'Lenin, October and the Union'.

But there were negative phenomena at work. Some were technical — from lack of facilities in the archives to paper shortages and plummeting academic salaries — but a political phenomenon also intruded into the process. Not all the archives were accessible. In particular, the materials gathered in the Kremlin by Valeri Boldin for the benefit of Mikhail Gorbachev contained a mass of highly important and sensitive documentation on the years between 1917 and 1991. These became known as the Presidential Archive and, although occasional textual reproductions were published from them, in general only a tiny circle of scholars was allowed to inspect and quote from them. The promise to restore the materials from the Presidential Archive to the archives from which they had been removed by Boldin has yet to be fulfilled.

The explanation, at least in part, appears to be a wish by government authorities to maintain leverage over public debate on the Soviet past. Boris Yeltsin's speeches from 1991 have been peppered with assertions about historical events and processes; and although he and his advisers have not attempted to replace a single Marxist-Leninist orthodoxy with a single Yeltsinite orthodoxy, they have indicated a distinct interpretative preference.

Perhaps the leading proponent of this preference is Dmitri Volkogonov, until recently a close adviser to Yeltsin, who in 1994 produced his biography *Lenin*, which drew directly upon the Presidential Archive. His devastating denunciation of Lenin was coupled with an analysis stressing that the terror regime established after the October Revolution was maintained by Stalin, Krushchev and Brezhnev. In short, Volkogonov is out to show that the entire Soviet period was an unalleviated nightmare for the peoples of the Soviet Union.

Volkogonov's interpretation is hardly new: even before 1991 there were writers who sought to pull Lenin from his pedestal. One of them, Vladimir Soloukhin, evinced a strident Russian nationalism in his pamphlet, *Reading Lenin*. Unlike Volkogonov, Soloukhin makes no plea for political democracy and a tolerant culture.

Others, however, have objected to the whole emphasis given by both Volkogonov and Soloukhin to simple, black-and-white explanations of the Soviet past. Some are unreconstructed Communist historians; some are semi-reconstructed or are writers who have seized on the opportunity presented by the collapse of Communism to demonstrate that the past was extraordinarily complex. An example of this is the short book *Stalin and Ordzhonikidze* by the youngish historian Oleg Khlevnyuk. His chapters trace the tensions in the Central Party leadership in the years leading up to the Great Terror of 1937-1938. He looks at the entanglement of political, economic and foreign policy issues confronting the Politburo at the beginning of the decade, and shows that alternative strategies were canvassed inside the supreme political leadership.

Such a work marks an attempt to move away from visions of the past glimpsed exclusively through the ideas and activities of the single leader of any given period. Khlevnyuk alludes to a wide set of decision-making forums and, in doing so, he and others of his ilk are implicitly questioning whether absolutely all the ills of the Soviet period were attributable to single leaders and the ideology they served. For there is an obvious temptation for readers of Soloukhin to assume that, if Lenin and Marxism-Leninism caused all the hardship, then Russians as a people were in

President Boris Yeltsin: history in the telling

no way culpable at any stage. Khlevnyuk, by contrast, asks Russians not to regard themselves simply as a martyred people. Many Russians, after all, persecuted, oppressed and killed other Russians.

A vibrant discussion is taking place. Needless to say, it is very polemical, at times as polemical as the debates among the revolutionaries in the tsarist period. It is occurring in the context of freer discourse, research and publication than at any time in the history of the country, even if those conditions remain far from ideal. Not everything adduced for discussion, moreover, is couched in harsh language. For example, the historian of the peasantry, M M Gromyko, has produced a book, *The World of the Russian Village* which recapitulates the lost customs, beliefs and working practices of the pre-revolutionary peasant. The pictures and diagrams in the book evoke a wonderfully harmonious age before the onset of Communism.

In fact the peasantry were sometimes as nasty to each other as the Bolsheviks eventually became to each other. But this is not the point. In painting an idealistic portrait, Gromyko has joined the throng of writers seeking to put the people back into their own history. There will be no end to debate, and personal jealousies and political rivalries will continue to bedevil scholarship on Mother Russia's past. So long as the plurality of viewpoint is maintained, the danger of an intolerantly monolithic version of the past re-emerging to justify present political purposes will stay small. ❑

YURI AFANASEV

Return history to the people

The parallel version of history that emerges from the testimony of eye witnesses is, of necessity, incomplete: many of those who could have contributed were killed by the regime. But it can fill gaps in the versions handed down by the authorities and frequently provides the perfect counterpoint to the myths propagated by the Soviet school. Nor is it above propounding a few dangerous myths of its own.

The study of this oral tradition has only recently been authorised and is centred in the Russian State University for the Humanities in the study group for oral history, run by Daria Khoudovïa. The most striking thing about the oral history of the Russian people is that it is immeasurably more truthful than official history: by and large, the anecdotes remain far more faithful to the facts than the Bolshevik version.

1) Official account of the Bolshevik victory in Moscow, November 1917

Young workers fought in the armed insurrection with unfailing courage. Numerous young people gave their lives in the struggle for the Soviets... To help save the workers of Moscow lined up against the tsarist cadet corps, Lenin called for reinforcements from Petrograd and on 1 November 2,000 sailors and Red Guards took up their positions outside the city. The Kremlin was surrounded and bombarded with artillery fire. At dawn on 3 November, the cadets laid down their arms. The insurrection had triumphed.

Recollections of a witness, aged 16

At the time we were living in a house which happened to be directly in the line of fire, near the Borovitsky Gate. With the battle raging outside, we couldn't leave; but neither could we stay in our apartments, with all the flying glass. So we were confined to the stairwells, to steps and landings and lobbies, crammed in together with our next of kin, our neighbours and all kinds of guests sitting on pillows and mattresses... We ate, we slept, the adults played cards... A volunteer from the Red Guard had dragged her piano out here. She had draped huge curtains over the windows and played tunes from the opera. I've no idea how long this lasted; it may have been five days... We were cheerful, carefree... We sang and danced...

I can see them now, the morning after the first night of battle, dressed in their leather jackets, crackshots from the Latvian corps, mostly... And in the midst of this crowd, an interminable line of students and cadets laying down their arms and ammunition before being led away by the Red Guard...*

The shooting had left many casualties. All schoolchildren were obliged by decree to come to the funeral... A huge procession made its way to the Kremlin walls to bury the Bolsheviks... Some people were trampled... As for the cadets, no one bothered to bury them.

2) A Stalinist historian's account of collectivisation

The toiling peasantry was always deeply aware of the necessity for collectivisation, under the guidance of the Communist Party which progressively and methodically paved the way for the transfer of the masses to collective farms. From the autumn of 1929, villages and whole districts came forward to register at the collective farms, voluntarily accepting the change from the old-style production process to a new, socialist system of relations. The watershed came in the second half of 1929, when the broad mass of the peasantry became persuaded of the advantages of collective agriculture... This allowed the Party to move on to a new stage in the political process: the liquidation of the *kulak* class. On 2 March 1930, the Politburo published Stalin's article 'The Giddy Heights of Success' which explained what Party policy in the countryside should be, emphasising the importance of voluntary decisions and condemning the exposure of peasants to administrative pressure.

Account given by a Cossack villager

In early December, the order was given to set up the collective farm and the entire stanitsa (traditional Cossack settlement) was renamed the Ilich kolkhoz. *The president told us that it had all been decided at the meeting: everyone was to join. People were afraid; deeply afraid. They said that a commune would be organised and that everyone would have to sleep side by side with two strapping great blokes at either end of the bed-covers. It really was frightening: the idea of everyone in the same house, under the same blanket. Terrible. But it was the earth and the livestock which caused us most anxiety. How we wept when they came to collect*

---

* This title was used by the Soviets to designate wealthy peasant landowners whom they had marked down for liquidation as 'class enemies'.

the animals. *They told us to bring them out of the cowshed, but no one wanted to do it. It was always an outsider who undertook the job. One of my aunts got hold of a pitch-fork and prevented them from taking her two horses. The next day they came to deport her, leaving the two children on their own… Then suddenly they said that Stalin's head had been turned by so much success and the plan was reversed… Those who didn't want to stay in the* kolkhoz *only had to take back their animals. Two months on, somebody had recovered a cow, someone else had got his mare back… But the animals were in bad shape: the herd was starving to death.*

3) Official account of the German occupation in World War II

The German army unleashed a virulent spate of anti–Soviet publicity; it propagated hatred of our country. Every soldier was instructed to kill anything Russian or Soviet, to have no pity on the old, women and children. From the earliest days of their incursion into Soviet territory, the Nazis embarked on a systematic massacre of the population. Soviet citizens, educated by the Party, organised courageous resistance to the occupying troops. The partisan movement — a shining example of the patriotism which galvanised the masses — was a source of great support to the Red Army.

A Belarusian peasant woman

There weren't many Germans in our village and they behaved well on the whole. If they didn't, we complained to the commander, who punished his soldiers. Naturally enough, they wanted to eat; they asked for eggs and bacon. Why not give it to them? They wanted to give us money which was worthless here… Sometimes they gave us sugar. They didn't want to take anything without paying. When they left, they told us that the Russians would be here in three days. I took the opportunity to join the partisans. Why tell a lie? I was afraid of the bombardments. My sister had spent the war in the forest with the Communists and the komsomol *people who hadn't been evacuated east. So long as there was enough to eat they were quiet, but when they got hungry they began to steal calves and hens. The peasants denounced them to the* Kommandatur. *The Germans organised a massive beat, caught nearly all of them and took them away to Germany.* ❏

© *Excerpted from* Ma Russie Fatale *(Calmann-Lévy, 1992)*
Translated by Irena Maryniak

Gorky Park, Moscow 1991: fallen idols, playground of history

A dialogue with history

What can history mean to a society that diligently forced the subject into a Procrustean bed for 70 years? In the Soviet Union, the past was treated according to the laws of Ptolemy. Historical ideas were simple and comfortable: the sun rose and circled the earth. The victories of socialism were equally clear-cut and, furthermore, underpinned by the Constitution. History textbooks were stuffed with the residue of Lenin's and Stalin's ideas, and well seasoned with Marx and Engels. Paradoxically, history itself became a science, with formulae and hypotheses that served as axiomatic truths requiring no evidence to support them. The fact that

Soviet society no longer demanded this evidence is itself symptomatic. *A Short Course on the History of the USSR* (ed Shestakov, 1937) became our logarithm table. With it, we sought to 'verify harmony', as they say, and measure life itself. Generations learned its contents by rote, like a religious text.

The task of rebuilding history is being undertaken with the help of previously unknown and secret documents. Selected materials from the state archives were released at the end of the 1980s, previously closed sources became more accessible, the publication of documents and monographs based on archival sources grew more widespread. But the real difficulty is grasping the skills and research techniques of a culture of dialogue.

A New History has arrived...able to penetrate the depths of daily existence and perceive the mechanisms of change in all walks of life

For years our study of historians resembled the methods of police investigators rather than scholars. We did not enter into an equal dialogue with our sources but interrogated them, giving ourselves the prerogative of passing judgement. As a result, many research historians have found themselves unprepared for the avalanche of information available today. We must not only renew and refresh our knowledge of history, but also ascertain its meaning.

A New History has arrived, equipped with the requisite modern apparatus, approaches and methodologies, infused with a new spirit of professional historiography. It is a history able to penetrate the depths of daily existence and perceive the mechanisms of change in all walks of life. We can judge the speed of these changes by comparison with developments in French historiography. It took 50 years for the new-style French historical research to reach a wider public. Time itself has speeded up today: we do not have 50 years to travel that same distance. ❑

Excerpted from the forthcoming Rossiya: XX Vek *(Russia: The Twentieth Century) edited by Yuri Afanasev, a five-volume collection of articles representing the thinking of the new historians (Russian State Humanitarian University)*

Translated from the Russian by Irena Maryniak

FROM THE KGB FILES

The birth of *samizdat*

The last few years have seen the appearance among the intelligentsia and our young people of certain ideologically corrupting documents in the form of political, economic and philosophical essays, literary works, open letters to government, Party, the judiciary or prosecutor, and memoirs written by those claiming to be 'victims of the personality cult'. Those who write and distribute these texts call them 'literature outside censorship' or *samizdat* [self-publishing].

These documents, presenting certain faults in the Communist system as though they were intrinsic flaws, misrepresent the history of the Communist Party of the Soviet Union and the Soviet state, criticise measures taken by the Party on the nationalities question and on economic and cultural development, make propaganda with opportunist theories on 'improvements' in socialism in the USSR, and end with demands for the abolition of censorship and the rehabilitation of those who have been condemned for anti-Soviet agitation.

In most cases, this *samizdat* is a typed or hand-written manuscript, passed from hand to hand and reproduced on photocopiers and duplicating machines. The distribution of these works attracts shady types and speculators who make a profit by selling them and holding on to the proceeds.

The propaganda disseminated in these *samizdat* is concocted in the course of all kinds of semi-official discussions — at musical evenings, at concerts, in clubs and even in the writers' unions. Many such organisations are led by people who have given no proof of their political soundness.

One should note that the preparation and distribution of these *samizdat* takes place dominantly in Moscow, but also in Leningrad, Kiev, Odessa, Novossibirsk, Gorky, Riga, Minsk, Kharkov, Sverdlovsk, Karaganda, Iouno-Sakhalinsk, Obninsk and in other towns and regions.

In Moscow, the preparation and distribution of these slanderous texts is done by individuals well known for their antisocial activities: Grigorenko, Litvinov, Bogoraz-Brouxman, Iakir. Grigorenko, in particular, wrote and took to the praesidium of the consultative meeting of representatives of Communist and workers' parties in Budapest a letter misrepresenting the creation of a Communist society by the CPSU. Litvinov and Bogoraz-Brouxman prepared and distributed an 'Appeal to world opinion' in which they accused the Soviet judicial system of violating the law. Iakir, in collaboration with other writers, put out an 'Appeal to men of learning, culture and the arts' containing fabrications on the 'restoration of Stalinism in the USSR'...

Some of these *samizdat* demand particular attention: the 'philosophical' article 'Reflections on progress, peaceful coexistence and intellectual freedom' by the academician Sakharov, the book by Medvedev, a researcher at the academy of pedagogical sciences...the notes, 'Letters to an unknown', by Iakoubovitch, a former Menshevik, now retired and living in Karaganda... These anti-Soviet and anti-social elements frequently send their 'uncensored' documents to western newspapers, magazines, radio stations and emigration centres hoping that by means of western broadcasts into the USSR, a significant number of Soviet citizens will come to know of their documents and that distribution will spread inside the country.

The information contained in their *samizdat* is largely used by capitalist intelligence organisations and foreign anti-Soviet groups in their campaigns against the USSR. They are presented by imperialist ideologues as 'proof' of an 'active opposition' inside the USSR. For instance, most recently, imperialist propaganda has made good use of the article by Sakharov and the work of Solzhenitsyn...

Imperialist reactionaries consider *samizdat* one of the ways in which they can weaken socialist society within our country and give the authors and distributors of these politically damaging documents all possible support. As a result, the print runs of books containing 'secret Soviet literature' have increased...

In addition to foreign publications and broadcasts into the country, there are other channels through which *samizdat* is brought into the USSR.

Given that the spread of a politically incorrect literature will affect the education of Soviet citizens, in particular our intelligentsia and our youth, the KGB are taking measures to suppress what the authors and disseminators of *samizdat* have done and limit the influence these 'uncensored' works have on the Soviet public. In 1968, the majority of those mixed up with *samizdat* — its writing as well as its distribution — were, with the help of social organisations, subjected to preventative interviews as a warning. Several who had made premeditated attacks on the Soviet state and its social system were brought before tribunals. ❏

Y V Andropov, president of the KGB, 7 February 1969

From the Centre for the Preservation of Contemporary Documentation Central Committee Archive, Moscow (fond 5, opis 69, delo 2890, pgs 86-88)

ALEXANDER BELY

What makes a Belarusian

The states newly liberated from Soviet control are making a hash of constructing their pre- and post-Soviet history

' Guess who it was? The greatest Polish poet, a Belarusian, of Jewish descent, who wrote "O Lithuania, land of my fathers!"?'

I was grateful for this question, put to his son by the father of a large Polish family when I was their guest in Warsaw. At least 90 per cent of Poles would consider the question an insult. Unfortunately, 90 per cent of today's average Belarusians would not even know of the existence of Mickiewicz, while the most fanatical Belarusian nationalist radicals take it for granted that Mickiewicz was not Polish at all and, indeed, was even an enemy of Poland because the Poles always oppressed Belarus!

For decades we were taught that there was no Belarusian history, except for the heroic deeds of the Communist resistance groups during World War II. Until recently, our only national hero was the leader of one such group who was sent from Russia. Whom shall we blame for this? Moscow? Or those *indigenes* who wrote about his 'immortal feats' and the oh-so-happy life on the collective farms?

Show-case patriots. Professional patriots. Patriotism to be paid for or rendered in kind. They simply switched a tumbler from one position to another — click! One fine day they found themselves ardent patriots of Belarus (or Croatia, Serbia, Russia, Chechnya — what you will) as they had formerly been adherents of Communism. In neither case was the ardour more than skin-deep.

Now, 80-year-old brochures with names like: *What Every Belarusian Should Know?* are being dusted off and republished. Updated catechisms called *100 Questions and Answers on Belarusian History* appear one after another. But, as before, it is once again a matter of the *correct* answers to the *correct* questions. Never mind that many names, dates and figures are terribly confused or simply incorrect. The authors hurried to provide their hoped-for disciples with spiritual food. It is the easiest thing in the world to be a specialist on Belarusian history. Is today's offering the 78th or 79th article on Francis Skaryna or the 65th on Euphrosyne of Polotsk, or number 1,001 on the 'unique mentality of the Belarusians!'? Unique fate, too! We are the only people in Europe who have been eaten away from all sides by ruthless enemies! These also deprived us of our history. The new politically-correct patriots think they can inject our national identity into the population in this way. Or would it simply be an inferiority complex?

So here we are swapping insults across the border with Lithuania, with whom we once made up a single entity within the Grand Duchy of Lithuania. But now, our 'patriots' say, the *Zmudziny* (Lithuanians) were savages. We gave them books and culture and in return these thankless dastards stole our primordial name of 'Litva' to which they have no right.

Indeed, the Lithuanians do not appreciate how much the Old Belarusian language and culture meant for the Grand Duchy. Shall we follow their example? Imagine the two women before Solomon, arguing about who should get the bigger piece of the baby!

One of the most intelligent Belarusian intellectuals, living in Poland, Sokrat Janovic, recently said, 'Belarus has often been occupied by foreign invaders. Now we are living through the occupation of Belarus by ostensible Belarusians.' The ultra-patriots say the biggest danger for the country is being absorbed once again by Russia, so anyone who does not support us is a traitor!

A pretty kettle of fish! Our only options, it seems, are to admit there is no such country as Belarus (and never was) and to get back to the bosom of Russia, or to join the caste of effete humanitarian intellectuals who want to turn the country into one great theme park.

I am not in favour of either.

Who truly loved Germany — Hitler or Thomas Mann? Who was the sincere patriot of Georgia — Gamsakhurdia or Memardashvili?

Too many questions. Stupid ones. Not ones that should occur to a true Belarusian. Am I one at all? ❏

Translated by Vera Rich

IHNAT SAHANOVIC

СИЗИФЪ
ВСЕМИРНАЯ ИСТОРІЯ
БАНК "ИМПЕРІАЛ"

*'Sisyphus with the rock of Imperial
history' from* Svaboda

In search of a theory

In Soviet times, in Minsk, it was openly said among archaeologists and historians that 'it is our job to collect the facts, theirs in Moscow to draw the conclusions for us.' And that's how it was. The direction of research and the guidelines for its treatment were laid down in Moscow; historiography was directed and monitored by the Party. On top of that, access to some 50 per cent of the archive material on the Soviet period was closed.

In the Belarusian SSR, scholars accepted and popularised many historical theses in complete contradiction to the historical facts but in accordance with the ideological principles of Communism. These myths included: the existence of a single ancient 'Russian' ethnic entity that was the 'cradle' of the Belarusians, Russians and Ukrainians; an age-old yearning of the Belarusians for union with Russia, the exclusively 'progressive' nature of Moscow's policies towards neighbouring peoples, the 'reactionary' nature of the national-democratic movement in Belarus, the nationwide support in Belarus for the Bolsheviks, etc. Thus, for example, the most disastrous war waged by Muscovy against Belarus (1654-67) in which the Tsar's armies annihilated over half the population of Belarus, was called in both scholarly and popular works 'the war of liberation of the Belarusian people for unification with Russia'.

The collapse of the Soviet regime and the creation of the Republic of Belarus gave Belarusian historiography the chance to revise the established treatment of our country's past. No easy task given the heavy legacy of totalitarianism, the embryonic state of methodology and the lack of a learned journal devoted to the discipline. Research took off in all directions regardless of theory or methodology. All too often the end result — an endless stream of narrow monographs — was a complete waste of time and resources. It has, so far, proved impossible to produce a much needed general work covering the whole of Belarusian history.

The first years of existence of the Republic of Belarus have brought no signs of any substantial renewal in the humanities, nor any strengthening of democracy. Power has remained in the hands of the Communists and pro-Communists, who have no interest in the reconstruction of historical scholarship. The state founded two new journals with a historical slant: the *Belarusian Historical Journal* and *Belarusian Antiquity*; both are confined to didactic works and popularisations.

Furthermore, the state of historical scholarship in Belarus is exceptionally difficult. The research staff of the Academy of Sciences has been drastically reduced. The end of the Marxist-Leninist monopoly on methodology left a vacuum. Young researchers, suspicious of any theory, make a fetish of 'facts'. Lack of money has meant drastic cutbacks in library acquisitions of foreign journals, and the possibility of private contacts with western historians are extremely limited.

In the absence of any initiative or support from the state authorities, a group of young historians from the Institute of History of the Academy of Sciences of Belarus founded the *Belarusian Historical Review* at the end of 1994. They consider it vital to encourage methodological pluralism, until now unacceptable to the majority of our scholars, to raise the voice of Belarusian historians in the world and to acquaint Belarusian historians with the findings of western research. One of the most pressing needs is access to the experience of non-Marxist historiography in the West and methods of interdisciplinary research. Hence the journal has begun to publish translations of key works of western historians. Priority is given to texts on methodology, problems of ethnic- and nation-building processes, intellectual and cultural history and historical sub-disciplines.

Unfortunately, the appearance of the new journal was not welcome in official circles. Recent events suggest that in the near future, its status may change dramatically — to that of an illegal publication. ❑

Translated by Vera Rich

JEREMY SCOTT

Virtual history

Scholarship and teaching are essentially indivisible... academic freedom is the right of all the People. Justice Sugimoto, 1970
The Constitution empowers the State to give the People the education they require...creativity and ingenuity create a biased view. Justice Takatsu, 1974

History is a partial business. Conventional wisdom holds that the winning side has a stranglehold over what the chronicles pass on to posterity, and it is perhaps natural that the process boils down complexity into a straightforward division between saints and sinners — at least for populist consumption.

But the underdogs also have an entrée into the editing process. In Japan, school textbooks 50 years on from the Pacific War present a heavily expurgated view of not only the events of 1941-45, but also the tangled story of the advance into Manchuria, China and South East Asia, knowledge of which is indispensible for any rounded understanding of why Japan and the USA, amid countless mutual misunderstandings, went to war. And the rewriting goes further, as 'virtual reality' books in their dozens climb the bestseller lists portraying a Japan where military might is still an option, where Japan wins a second Gulf War, and in an extreme case — *Deep Blue Fleet*, by Yoshio Aramaki — where Pacific War Admiral Yamamoto is reincarnated in a parallel world, 'liberates' Hawaii from the US and destroys the Panama Canal.

The bestsellers are a new phenomenon, but the textbook problem has dogged Japan for 30 years. In 1966 a history text challenging established policy by filling in the hole left by the wartime years, by a Marxist historian, Saburô Ienaga, was gutted by the Education Ministry under its right to review and licence all textbooks used in public schools. Ienaga sued, and his case against the government remains mired in the Japanese legal system to this day amid the conflicting judgements which head this article.

Again in the 1980s, the Education Ministry got into hot water over its portrayal of Japan's past. Headlines claiming the Ministry had changed 'invade' (*shinryaku*) to 'advance' (*shinshutsu*) with reference to the war with China over Manchuria from 1937 onwards — and particularly the Rape of Nanjing, which saw the murder of 70,000 Chinese civilians — screamed from every Japanese newspaper in 1982, prompting a massive row with China and South Korea which both countries used to advantage in trade and economic negotiations.

In fact, the so-called 'textbook flap' of 1982 was a flop. The revision had never occurred in the sense suggested by the newspaper reports: it was the product of traditionally heavy-handed government news management, which customarily released the year's texts to education correspondents at such short notice that the task of scanning them was shared by the reporters amongst themselves — and a single error was repeated across the press as a whole.

The international repercussions of the textbooks, the bestsellers, the trucks laden with loudspeakers that tour Tokyo calling for Japan's imperial glory to be resurrected, and the apparent refusal to face the legacy of the war head on, stretch far beyond negotiating points. Japan fought the Pacific War on the basis of creating a Greater East Asia Co-Prosperity Sphere — a supposedly anti-colonial crusade, bringing the Pacific a golden age under Japanese guidance — and recent years have kindled a fear, principally in the USA, that that aim is effectively being realised under the guise of the new Asian industrialism.

For this reason President Clinton has ensured the USA a place at, for instance, the Asia Pacific Economic Cooperation forum (APEC) and Malaysia's prime minister, Mahathir Mohammed, is not alone in suggesting Japan as *primus inter pares* of a Pacific free trade area.

But if the Rape of Nanjing goes unrecognised in some circles, the thousands of Korean women forced into unpaid prostitution for their occupiers — known as 'comfort women' in Japanese — are without apology or reparation (see p151), and Japan has yet to make peace with Russia over the Kurile islands seized by the USSR in 1945 about which feelings in Japan run high. Coupled with the crippling effect of recession and the high yen on Japan's economy, this makes the prospect of 'Pax Nipponica' posited in the late 1980s a receding one.

On the face of it, Japan's inability or unwillingness to deal with the war seems to do it more harm than good; but there were cogent reasons for blotting out 15 years of history. One was the real desire among survivors of the war, largely thanks to the horror of Hiroshima and Nagasaki, to rebuild from scratch, to take Article 9 of the US-imposed constitution — that forbids Japan both aggression and its tools — at its word and construct a genuinely non-military state, although recent budgets have seen the cost of Japan's Self-Defence Force rise to rank among the world leaders.

Another lies in the fact that the occupying forces under General Macarthur, facing Communist China, let most of the wartime administrators and businessmen stay in place to make Japan a bulwark against Communism and ensure its survival through open access to US markets. Successive generations of Japanese elites have continued to exploit the niche they were handed, but that very continuity required that some things be kept out of circulation.

The resulting paradox: that continuity needs amnesia, that for Japan to have sustained its mobilisation towards economic success, it has had to forget the path taken to reach it. And the scars go way beyond international problems to affect all aspects of modern Japan. A UN Security Council seat would seem commensurate with Japan's economic role, but is enmeshed in the intractable debate over Article 9 and stationing peace-keeping forces overseas. A bureaucracy set up to run a near-command economy can find no institutional alternative to help it manage a deregulated, internationalist state — and the resulting administrative paralysis was clear in the response to offers of foreign assistance in the aftermath of the Kobe earthquake.

But the most significant damage is less direct. The years from 1931 to 1945 are a hole in the nation's psyche. On the most basic level, schoolchildren ask of the Pacific War, 'Who won?' but as postwar writers like Michiko Hasegawa complain of being 'born of nothingness', so the spiritual rootlessness left by extinguishing 15 years as an 'aberration' must find other places to earth itself. It does so in the right-wing soundtrucks. It does so in the inability to formulate an apology for the war acceptable to all sides of the disparate coalition government. It does so in the lingering taste among conservative politicians for visiting Yasukuni Shrine, where the remains of Japan's war dead, including several war criminals, are housed.

And it does so in the false security offered by the multiplying cults of which Oum Shinrikyô is only one, albeit extreme, example. Not only

On the streets of Tokyo: consumer history

the cult's recent activities, but also the credence given to its recent threat of a catastrophe worse even than Kobe, provide symptoms of a particularly virulent Japanese strain of millennialism, and its virulence is the direct product of psychic damage wrought by the burying of things past. The cults offer certainties, and the doctrine of economism which has both reinforced and been supported by 50 years of denial, which has taken the place of that which existed before, is now collapsing amid deregulation, competition and the turmoil of severe recession.

Rigidity — as demonstrated in April's economic package to combat the high yen, which disappointed the most modest expectations — has set in after half a century on a single course, and only recognition that its roots lie in its 15 missing years could spur Japan into dealing with the new realities. But the omens are not good for such a leap of faith. In this way Japan has paid and is paying for the war; and the payment seems set to remain in the path of a nation ill at ease with the world and with itself. ❏

ROBERT FISK

From Beirut to Bosnia

Despite the peace negotiations between Israelis and Palestinians in Israel, there is, it seems, no intention on the part of Jews or Arabs to reunite their own particular versions of each others' history

In 1993, Robert Fisk, Middle East correspondent of the London Independent *newspaper, appeared in a three-part film series called* Beirut to Bosnia *which was shown by Britain's Channel 4 television and in the United States last year by Discovery. Lebanon's NEW TV channel has also shown the films. But in the USA, a powerful Israeli lobby ensured there was no second showing of the films while in Lebanon, a fit of self-censorship ensured that viewers saw only a lobotomised version of the Holocaust*

We knew the campaign had started when the US Discovery channel reported that some of its advertisers were being pestered with telephone calls from supposedly outraged viewers. American Express, one of the channel's sponsors, received credit cards back from customers; the cards had been cut in half. An organisation calling itself 'Promoting Responsibility in Middle East Reporting' wrote to Discovery with a sinister warning. Robert Fisk had 'impeccable English diction', wrote Joseph I Ungar, the group's vice-president, in June 1994. Fisk projected 'the essence of refinement and respectability... He could easily play the stage role of Henry Higgins. But he could be a Higgins with fangs.'

In journalism, you have to laugh at this sort of rubbish. But the campaign against *Beirut to Bosnia* was not funny at all. The president of the same lobby organisation, Sidney Laibson, wrote a letter to John Hendruks, chairman of Discovery, the same month. 'By airing *Beirut to Bosnia*,' he wrote, 'the Discovery Channel has provided the purveyors of insidious propaganda an opportunity to spread their venom into the

Peace in Gaza, 1994: business of history

living-rooms of the USA.' The McCarthyite rhetoric has been familiar to me for years. I get mailbags full of this kind of rancour every time I write a report which does not reflect favourably upon Israel as Israel's supporters would like. The intention is always the same: to persuade me not to write anything critical of Israel or to persuade the editor of the *Independent* not to publish anything critical of Israel or — in the case of men like Mr Laibson and Mr Ungar — to prevent Discovery re-showing films like *Beirut to Bosnia*. And in the USA last year, they got their way.

Beirut to Bosnia was not an easy film series to make. We filmed in Lebanon, Gaza, Israel, Egypt, Bosnia and Croatia in an attempt to show — as the film said in its initial sequence — why so many Muslims had come to hate the West. In Lebanon, we questioned Hizbollah fighters about their war against Israeli occupation troops, asked their leader why young men suicide-bombed US marines and seized western hostages. Our cameras filmed women in Lebanese hospitals who were covered in burns from Israeli phosphorous shells. In Gaza, filming during Israeli curfews, we were repeatedly ordered off the streets by Israeli soldiers — several times, our crew filmed Israeli officers as they placed their hands over our camera lens. We filmed an Israeli officer who told us a pregnant Palestinian woman had been allowed throughout the curfew to go to hospital — then found the woman still trapped in her home. Outside the walls of Jerusalem, we talked to a Jewish settler who explained why an elderly Palestinian was being evicted from his land — because Jews would be living there and because, in the settler's words, 'he isn't an Arab'. In Israel, we traced the home of a Palestinian refugee now living in Beirut, talked to the elderly Israeli who moved into the house after 1948 — and took our cameras to the Polish town from which he fled and from which his parents and brother were taken by the Nazis to be murdered in the Holocaust.

I get mail bags full of rancour every time I write a report which does not reflect favourably upon Israel

In Egypt, we interviewed supporters of the Gema'a Islamiya, the violent Islamist group fighting the Egyptian government and attacking western tourists. And in Sarajevo, we talked to front-line Muslim fighters and to the Imam of Bosnia; we visited the burned home of a Muslim family 'ethnically cleansed' by the Serbs in northern Bosnia. And we ended the third film among newly 'cleansed' Muslims as they waited in despair on a Croatian railway platform for their journey to the ends of the earth.

During the filming, we were threatened by government officials in Egypt, sniped at and under repeated shellfire in Bosnia, harassed in Gaza. We used real film, which is far more expensive than videotape. And we abjured the time-worn 'stand-upper' where the reporter plays the traditional role of talking to the viewer. In these films, the camera followed me as I went about my work for the *Independent*. We used none of the traditional clichés. The word 'terrorist' did not appear in the script.

In Britain, viewers who were sympathetic to Israel objected to any Muslim militant being given a voice on the programme, but reaction was otherwise muted. Newspaper reviewers were generally favourable, the

Observer noting how rarely the suffering of Lebanese civilians wounded by Israeli shellfire was seen on British screens. In the USA, however, there was a quite different response.

On 27 April 1994, on the eve of Discovery's coast-to-coast showing of the films, the *New York Times* carried a prominent review of the series which included some apparently wilful distortions. In his review, Walter Goodman claimed that 'most of the three-hour report concentrates on Palestinians,' and that I had made only what he called 'references' to the Holocaust. This was untrue. Less than a third of the series dealt with Palestinians, and we had covered the story of the Israeli family's suffering in the Holocaust, filming not only in their former Polish home town but at the site of Treblinka extermination camp. These sequences were not mere 'references'. I wrote to the *New York Times*, asking them to correct these errors of fact. Without explanation, they refused to do so.

Then, only days after Discovery showed the three films coast-to-coast, the letter-writing campaign began. Discovery's letter from Joseph Ungar claimed that for us to say that Israel 'confiscates', 'occupies' and 'builds huge Jewish settlements on Arab land' — all facts acknowledged by Israeli human rights groups as well as by foreign correspondents for many years — was 'twisted' history. A reference in my commentary to the 'Christian gunmen' that the Israelis 'sent' into the Sabra and Chatila camps before the massacre in 1982 — a course of events detailed in Israel's own Kahan Commission judicial report — was condemned by Mr Ungar as 'an egregious falsehood'. Despite the absolute proof provided by our cameras and soundtrack, Mr Ungar denied that the Palestinian woman had been refused permission to go to hospital during the Gaza curfew. We had not substantiated that the woman was pregnant, he asserted, nor that there was a curfew. The woman in fact gave birth to her child that summer — we later visited the baby — while the curfew was self-evident. The soldier on the film specifically ordered us to leave because there was a curfew. But the films, Ungar concluded, were 'artful', 'diabolically clever'; the series was 'filled with dark echoes' and 'should never been (sic) aired by Discovery'.

Alex Safian of the Camera Media Resources Centre wrote to Clark Bunting, senior vice-president of Discovery, on 9 June 1994. He claimed that an edited sequence showing Micki Molad, the settler we interviewed outside Jerusalem, had included a remark by him that Jews originally owned most of the land for the future settlement. Michael Dutfield, the

Beirut to Bosnia: Fisk with Hamas supporter in South Lebanon

director of the series, ran back through the rough-cuts, to all the sequences — almost an hour of them — in which Molad had spoken to us. And in the sequence in which Safian claimed Molad had made this remark, the settler actually said: 'Now we were talking, Bob — and you were asking me — about Arabs and Jews, and here I'll let you understand a bit about the geography.' Safian's claims, Dutfield wrote back, were 'absurd and demonstrably wrong'.

Safian's letter also claimed that the episode of the pregnant woman 'may have been staged for the camera' because in an article on the same incident in the *Independent* I had referred to the woman's brother-in-law as bearded when the film clearly shows him to be clean-shaven. In fact, the film shows him bearded, just as I described him in the article.

While this campaign of calumny was going on in the USA — and while Dutfield was refuting in detail every falsehood contained in the letters — Lebanon's NEW TV network purchased the right to the films and aired them in Beirut in late 1994. Arab television is notoriously subject to censorship or self-censorship — even in Lebanon — but I was assured by the directors that there would be no changes made in the films. In fact, several deletions were made in the first two films. A reference to Syria's 20,000-strong army in Lebanon was taken out of the first, my laconic comment that God — the subject of an immediately preceding interview with a Palestinian — was apparently sending Yasser Arafat to help his people, was deleted from the second.

Far more important, however, was that the second film lost almost the entire Holocaust sequence. The sequences of the Palestinians remained untouched but the moment our cameras arrived at the home of the Palestinian refugee in Haifa and the Israeli who now lives there began to speak, the screen image jerked and the television closed down the film with advertisements. The old Israeli's story, the photographs of his murdered parents, the filmed sequences in Poland and Treblinka, were all excised. The Holocaust, in the Lebanese version of the film, had indeed become a 'reference'. When I complained bitterly about this to one of the television company's officials, he replied that 'the security people here (in Lebanon) don't like things about Jews and Poland.'

There is no evidence that the 'security people' in Lebanon have ever expressed a view on the Holocaust or World War II or indeed on any aspect of Jewish history. Indeed Lebanon, of all Arab countries, was the only one to allow Jews to work in its civil service after the 1948 war. But only after further complaints to the management of the television station did I elicit a promise to reinsert the Holocaust sequence in the second showing of the film series. Which they did, as promised. The film was shown in its entirety. It was, I believe, the first time that documentary footage on the Holocaust had been shown on Arab TV.

But at least in Lebanon there was a second showing. Not so in the USA. Several colleagues of mine had already warned me of the sequence of events that was likely to follow the airing in the USA of any film which did not present Israel as a heroic nation standing alone as a beacon of western democracy against Arab 'terrorists'. First, they said, Discovery would fail to defend the films, despite the absolute proof that the allegations against the series were lies. Secondly, I would hear from viewers that Discovery had cancelled a second showing because of the number of 'inaccuracies' in the series which would be discovered by supposedly independent media groups.

And so it came to pass. When the original, spurious allegations were sent to the television network, Discovery had made no attempt to defend the films. A forthright rebuttal of the claims would, at least, have shown that the US media, supposedly champions of free speech and honest journalism, were not going to be intimidated. On the contrary, Discovery's 'viewer relations' department wrote back to Sidney Laibson in June 1994, with the observation that 'your letter is important to us and has been forwarded to the appropriate department for further review.'

What this 'appropriate department' was I have been unable to discover. But on 22 February 1995, I received the first letter of which I had been warned, from a woman reader of the *Independent*. She had, she said, asked 'American friends' about the reaction to *Beirut to Bosnia*. These 'friends' told her that 'there had been numerous complaints because of a number of serious inaccuracies in the film...which eventually led to the network cancelling a scheduled re-airing of the series.'

I wrote to Dutfield, requesting him to ask Discovery if this was true. Back came a reply, this time from Clark Bunting, the senior vice-president. '...given the reaction to the series upon its initial airing,' he replied, 'we never scheduled a subsequent airing, so there is not really an issue as to any scheduled re-airing being cancelled.' This extraordinary and gutless remark was followed by an assertion from Bunting that 'we have not stated that there are factual inaccuracies in the series.'

The phraseology was important. Discovery, instead of standing by its reporters, merely 'did not state' that there were 'factual inaccuracies'. And Mr Bunting, apparently missing the point of his own remark, suggested that no 'issue' was involved because — as he states quite clearly — the 'reaction' (from Messrs Laibson and others) was such that no re-showing of the film was scheduled.

In a masterpiece of understatement, Dutfield replied that while he did not seek to question Discovery's 'broadcasting policy', he was 'concerned...that your reply, by failing to support the series, might give comfort to those who seek to restrict the legitimate and entirely necessary debate about the Middle East. There are groups who seek to intimidate broadcasters out of contributing to that debate and many of those who have objected to this series belong to those groups.'

There is, of course, no recourse to any journalistic fair play here. Commercial-political pressure drove *Beirut to Bosnia* — which showed Muslims as victims rather than aggressors — off US screens because Israel's friends did not like it. A refusal to see Jews as victims rather than aggressors persuaded the Lebanese to censor the Holocaust. The USA and Lebanon have more in common than they realise. In the end however, maybe Lebanon has something to teach the USA. ❏

MINORITIES

Reclaiming the Dreamtime

'History has changed how our people look at themselves. When the whites came to this country, they didn't make treaties, they started raping and killing and poisoning. They brought in alcohol, muskets, sabres, strychnine, the flogging whip and chains. We'd never had hell before. Everything in this sacred land had been sacred and we were one with all created life until white savages came and called us "black apes" and "primitive". It's past now but we are products of the past. Our people have forgotten that there was a time when our men fought them and fought well...in the days before our soul was crushed.'

Adelaide 1988: no cause for celebration

Grandfather Koori from *Living Black* compiled by Kevin Gilbert

There was little for Aboriginals to celebrate in Australia's bicentennial jamboree in 1988 that commemorated the arrival of the first white settlers. Since the Englishman Captain James Cook first 'discovered' their continent in 1770, they have been systematically robbed of their land, their culture and their dignity. In the nineteenth century they were hunted down like animals for a Sunday's sport and, with their land gone, were herded into 'missions'; for much of this century, the government took small children away from their families in an attempt to eradicate all knowledge of Aboriginal language and culture. This was the 'lost generation' of a 'dying people': a race the white settlers determined to expunge from history.

And failed. From the beginning, the Aboriginals fought back against overwhelming odds. In 1967 they won citizenship and the last 20 years have seen an unprecedented Aboriginal initiative demanding political and cultural rights and, above all, recognition of their right to their lands and sacred places. Today they have legal equality but continue to suffer discrimination and persecution in most fields: infant mortality is three times higher, suicide rates six times higher, prisoners 14 times greater and life expectancy 18 years shorter than the national average.

What Kevin Gilbert calls 'the rape of the Aborigine soul' was so profound the blight continues in the mind of most blacks today. Their continuing fight is for more than land: it is for the return of their history, their soul. ❏ *Research by Atanu Roy*

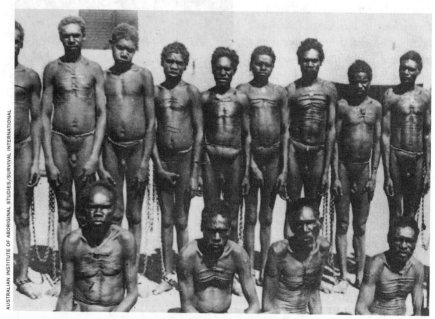

Kimberley, West Australia 1906: 'they bought the flogging whip and chains'

Pitjabjantarra county, Central Australia: Aboriginal land protest

In 1995, legal proceedings for reparation were initiated in the Australian courts. Almost 70 years after she was removed from her mother, Hilda Muir began an action on behalf of herself and others of the 'stolen generation', victims of a forced policy of assimilation operated from the 1920s to 1960s. She claims the policy breached the Australian Constitution and the International Genocide Convention and demands that it be ruled invalid. If successful, the case could lead to thousands of demands for personal, cultural and spiritual loss. After years of litigation, the UK has agreed to pay around US$30 million in compensation for the contamination of Aboriginal land and people during atomic tests in the 1950s. Compensation for the lost lands is still to be won.

'Aboriginals see themselves as part of nature and all things on earth as part human.' For 40 millennia and more, the Aboriginal people lived in a delicate ecological balance with a harsh environment. The land is sacred, essential to their physical and metaphysical survival; their relationship to it rooted in the Dreamtime, a time long past when the earth was first created. Two hundred years ago, the white man decreed their land to be terra nullius: uninhabited, virgin and therefore open to the settlers' claims. The Aboriginals lost all title and were driven from the sacred places of their dreaming. Aboriginal title was finally recognised in 1992 but their land is still not their own: the land remains at risk from tourism, development and, above all, mining.

81

Alice Springs, Central Australia: an Aranda elder with children at Yippirringa Dreaming place

'At the white man's school, what are our children taught?
Are they told of the battles our people fought,
Are they told of how our people died?
Are they told why our people cried?
Australia's true history is never read,
But the blackman keeps it in his head.'

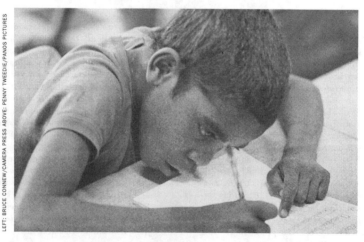

Learning the white man's way

In sickness and in Dreaming

'Then they got the pox, syphilis, gonorrhoea, colds, pneumonia, TB that the whiteman's ships brought in.' Even today, white Australia has done little to cure the diseases it inflicted. Systematic neglect, vicious discrimination, insanitary and overcrowded housing and exclusion from the national health system ensure that diseases all but eradicated elsewhere persist among the Aboriginal community.

Aboriginal pride: pictures of the soul

Shopping expedition in Alice Springs

With the help of satellite technology, Aboriginal broadcasting now reaches round their world. The Central Australian Aboriginal Media Association broadcasts in Aboriginal languages from Alice Springs. Its TV franchise was won in open competition with other Australian commercial stations.

Brisbane 1982: arrest during land rights demonstration

ISAAC DEUTSCHER LECTURE

HARVEY J KAYE

Why do ruling classes fear history?

ISAAC DEUTSCHER LECTURE

1989 was the two-hundredth anniversary of the French Revolution, and — contrary to the schemes of the governing classes, West and East — developments of that year seemed to provide dramatic living proof that the grand ideals of 1789 were not just remembered but still inspiring and informing action. Across Eurasia and beyond, struggles for liberty, equality and democracy asserted themselves. Rebellions claimed control of public spaces and toppled rulers and regimes. There were triumphs like the tearing down of the Berlin Wall, and there were tragedies like the Tiananmen Square massacre. But, together, these events reminded people globally of the popular desire for freedom and the demand for power to the people! There was reason to celebrate and to believe more was yet to come.

And yet, within just a few years the hope and sense of possibility engendered by those events and the end of the Cold War have been overtaken by other, darker developments and the spiritual order of the day has become one of despair and cynicism. Emulating the most brutal traditions of this 'age of extremes' (as Eric Hobsbawm has dubbed the twentieth century), the politics of the new world order are apparently dominated by greed, hatred, and mass murder — sadly, I need merely mention Somalia, Bosnia, Rwanda. European life is marked by resurgent nationalisms, fascisms, xenophobia and, most bizarrely, in view of the tragic success of the Nazis to rid the continent of Jews, anti-Semitism.

At the same time — and surely contributing in massive proportion to the reinvigoration of the former — the market now rules globally, North and South, subsuming everything and everyone to the command of capital, intensifying already gross inequalities as the rich grow richer and working people poorer, and ever threatening to completely destroy the western labour movement and its finest twentieth-century achievement, social-democratic government. It becomes less and less possible to gain a hearing for the 'public good' or 'commonweal'.

Public discourse and private thoughts across the political spectrum seem to accept — as the US neo-conservative, Francis Fukuyama, put it — that we are at 'the end of history'. With the global triumph of capitalism we are believed to have arrived at the terminus of world-historical development, the culmination of universal history, entailing not only the collapse of the Soviet Union but the consignment of *all* varieties of socialism (assuming you could ever call the Soviet system socialist) to the graveyard of history. Fundamentalisms and particularisms may arise to challenge liberal capitalism as is already happening — but there is no universal alternative to it now or in the future. In fact, Edward Lutwak's recent survey of the world makes Fukuyama's own thesis seem downright optimistic for, in place of liberalism, he sees 'Fascism as the Wave of the Future'. In any case, radical-democratic possibilities are finished; the further progress and development of liberty and equality is foreclosed, forever. To think otherwise is declared, and widely perceived to be, not just utopian but dangerous.

I do not accept that assumption, and I will not defer to it. We are not fulfilled and our requirements and satisfactions are not simply material. History and its progressive political possibilities are not resolved.

Still, I take the 'end of history' most seriously. I do so not merely because the appearance of Fukuyama's audacious work was a smartly-timed literary and commercial coup orchestrated with the financial support of a corporately-endowed New Right foundation, but because — however illusory a notion it really is — it has articulated anew the perennial ambitions and dreams of the powers that be to make their regimes and social orders not just omnipotent and universal, but immortal. And, at least for now, it does seem to capture in a single phrase the dominant historical vision.

To those of us who still aspire to advance the critical and democratic ideals of the Enlightenment and Age of Revolution, the old question — *What is to be done?* — continues to present itself. And yet, there would

Movable icons, Berlin 1945: Stalin's portrait replaces Hitler's throughout East Germany

seem to be an even prior and more urgent question: from where can we draw sustenance, hope, and a sense of possibility when, admittedly, there are substantial reasons to be pessimistic? Most immediately, I can do no better than to quote the great socialist intellectual, Isaac Deutscher: 'Awareness of historical perspective seems to me,' he wrote, 'to provide the best antidote to extravagant pessimism as well as extravagant optimism over the great problems of our time.'

... It is my contention that however imposing their power, and however acquiescent may seem the people over whom they exercise it, the eyes of the ruling classes reflect not surety and confidence, but apprehension and anxiety. *What* is it that they see? *What* is it that they recognise? *What* is it that they know?...

In the looks and actions of the powerful, we may discover what exercises them so and, at the same time, be reminded of what we appear to be on the verge of forgetting. Ultimately, we will have to ask: *Why do ruling classes fear history?*

... Clearly distinguishing between 'the past' as ideological construct and 'history' as critical knowledge, in *The Death of the Past* J H Plumb succinctly summarises the parade of ruling-class elaborations and uses of the former from ancient to recent times: 'The past was constantly involved in the present; and all that enshrined the past — monuments, inscriptions, records were essential weapons in government, in securing the authority, not only of the king, but also of those whose power he symbolised and sanctified...'

Plumb may have underestimated the persistence of the past today, and the continuing ambitions and efforts of elites to compose and direct it, but he appreciated its essential significance: 'Myths and legends, king-lists and genealogies... Whig-interpretations and Manifest Destinies... All rulers needed an interpretation of the past to justify [and sanctify] the authority of their government... The past has always been the handmaid of authority.'

Our own century is hardly free of such practices. Subscribing to the Party's slogan in Orwell's *1984* — 'Who controls the past controls the future; who controls the present controls the past' — totalitarian and authoritarian regimes have ceaselessly sought to dominate and manipulate public and private memory. It was true of Nazism and Fascism, it was true of Communism, and it has been true of a great host of pettier, though not necessarily meeker, dictatorships.

Compared to the devastations of blitzkrieg and conquest and the organised murder of 6,000,000 Jews, book burnings and perversions of the past seem minor crimes, but they should never be discounted, for the Nazis' criminal treatment of history served to rationalise and justify to the German people their later crimes against humanity. Those today who deny that the Holocaust ever happened may be exercising their right of free speech (and demonstrating that ruling classes do not have an absolute monopoly on trying to suppress the past), but they are also committing atrocities against memory and history (see p43). The presence in Europe's streets of neo-Nazis, along with the re-ascendance of fascist politicians, is chilling.

Censorship in the Soviet Union began under Lenin as a 'temporary measure'. However, as David Remnick writes in *Lenin's Tomb*: 'The Kremlin took history so seriously that it created a massive bureaucracy to control it, to fabricate its language and content, so that murderous and arbitrary purges became a 'triumph over enemies and spies', and the reigning tyrant, a 'Friend to All Children'.

Isaac Deutscher gives accounts in his biographies of Stalin and Trotsky of how, early on in Stalin's campaigns against his rivals, he 'started the prodigious falsification of history which was to descend like a destructive avalanche upon Russia's intellectual horizons' and of how, by the onset of the 1930s, he was requiring falsehoods and cover-ups ever more massive. Show trials, purges, famines, deportations, concentration camps, murders in their millions... Stalin and the Party imposed a grand 'conspiracy of silence'.

After more than a quarter century, the horrors and the lies, and the official suppression of any reference to them, were bound together so tightly that Stalin's successors could not afford to loosen the controls too much. How could they when they had all been his 'accomplices'? Krushchev himself fully appreciated the powers of the past and, ironically, offered one of the finest — though hardly universally deserved — tributes to the profession that I have ever come upon: 'Historians are dangerous and capable of turning everything topsy-turvy. They have to be watched.'

> **'Stalin...started the prodigious falsification of history which was to descend like a destructive avalanche upon Russia's intellectual horizon'**
> *Isaac Deutscher*

While the darkest days did not return, history remained under close supervision and regulation — with occasional 'thaws', followed regularly by 'purges' — until *glasnost* and *perestroika* in the mid-1980s. Yet, Gorbachev was no fool. Even he would have preferred, at least at the outset, not to extend the processes of opening and restructuring to questions of the past; indeed, it was not until he imagined that allowing public re-examination and revision of the historical record would help to undermine the opposition and thereby enable him to advance his bureaucratic and economic reforms that he called for the filling in of the all-too-many 'blank spots'.

Having been so well supervised, professional scholars were themselves at first hesitant about undertaking the now licensed re-examination of Soviet experience. But others were not, and very quickly the historical past was asserting itself everywhere. I distinctly remember the Soviet government's announcement late in May 1988 that, in view of the great changes underway, school history examinations were being cancelled. In time, more was to be cancelled than that.

Gorbachev's miscalculations — assuming he never actually intended the breakup of the Soviet Union — also invited the renewal and redemption of politics and history in eastern Europe. In 1988, on the twentieth anniversary of the Prague Spring and the crushing by Warsaw Pact tanks of the Czechoslovak experiment in socialist democracy, the dissident group, Charter 77, issued a statement which concluded with the following: 'We call only for truth. The truth about the past and the truth about the present are indivisible. Without accepting the truth about what happened it is impossible to address correctly what is happening now; without the truth about what is happening now it is impossible to substantially improve the existing state of affairs.' In the Baltic republics, political insurgency was accompanied by demands for complete disclosure of the 'secret protocols' of the 1939 Hitler-Stalin Pact which had sealed their fates. Similarly, ongoing political changes in Poland, pursued for so long by the workers and intellectuals of Solidarity, generated a series of historical 'revelations' regarding Soviet actions before, during and after World War II. And in Hungary, along with popular demands for political reform, a 'Committee for Historical Justice' was organised to pursue, in particular, the recovery of the buried past of the Revolution of 1956. Submerged since 1945, extreme-nationalist and reactionary forces reasserted themselves in each of these instances, threatening in their respective fashions to replace the Communist suppression of memory and history with nationalist repressions. Nevertheless, the importance of history to the liberation movements of 1989 authenticated the words of the Czech novelist, Milan Kundera, that 'The struggle of man against power is the struggle of man against forgetting.'

Further east, the Communist Chinese leadership, in spite of all their revolutionary designs, actually renewed their imperial forerunners' management of the past and those who studied it. In fact, Mao and his cadres, in the words of Jonathan Unger, were: 'Even more determined to control the messages imparted in works of history — to bend those messages in ways favourable to official policy lines and to extirpate any manifestation of dissent or opposition that might be hidden in historical allegory... Historians, in short, were to serve as handmaidens to the Party propagandists'.

The degree of control exercised since 1949 has varied, though obviously not as much as the historiographical directions dictated by the government's changing political and economic policies. For their part, Chinese historians and other producers of 'the past' have themselves occasionally, though unsuccessfully, spoken up for the 'right to remember' — as in the spring of 1989 when, in a petition supporting the students and workers mobilising in Tiananmen Square, a group of writers in Shanghai called for the right to pursue 'free historical enquiry'. However, following the events of the night of 4 June there came the predictable ideological backlash, commencing with the government's propaganda machine describing the army's violent suppression of the democracy movement as actions taken against 'counter-revolutionaries'.

Before World War II, Japanese education was an instrument of indoctrination, cultivating in children the belief that the nation's overseas expansion was a sacred campaign to bring the 'whole world under one roof'; and, in order to guarantee that they promoted 'loyalty to the emperor and love of country', all textbooks were subject to certification by the Ministry of Education. With defeat and the ensuing US occupation, educational practices were reformed and, within certain guidelines, teachers were permitted to choose their own texts. But this did not last long. By the 1950s, the conservative, Liberal–Democratic Party government was succeeding in reinstituting state controls on education and the authorisation of textbooks, against the opposition of the Teachers Union. Most problematically, this meant that, in spite of the growing scholarly historiography on the subject, the government was able to have removed from the history schoolbooks, specific references to the atrocities committed by the Imperial Japanese military during the World War II, most infamously, the 1937 'Rape of Nanking' (see p68). Due to persistent legal campaigns by liberals and leftists and, perhaps even more significantly, diplomatic wrangles with the governments of those East Asian countries that had suffered Japanese depredations, prohibitions have been reduced or withdrawn, but state control and censorship of the schoolbooks continues.

The distortion and occlusion of the historical past by governing elites has, to varying degrees, characterised public history and historical education in all of the former Axis countries, regularly with the

CAMERA PRESS

Japan surrenders 1945: the hidden face of public history

acquiesence, if not the encouragement, of their former opponents eagerly pursuing Cold War and anti-left ends. Consider the postwar politics of amnesia surrounding the Austrians' image of themselves as simply the 'victims' of German expansionism; and the 'historical' initiatives of conservative German Chancellor Helmut Kohl, ranging from the Bitburg ceremonies in 1985 to his recent plans to commemorate officially the fiftieth anniversary of the plot to assassinate Hitler which deliberately excluded representatives of the social-democratic and Communist anti-Nazi resistance movements. Here, we might also register the half-century worth of political prevarications and equivocations in France engendered by the nation's 'Vichy Syndrome'.

Whereas the archives have been opened in Berlin and Moscow; US and other western secrets about foreign and domestic, state and corporate crimes committed under licence of the Cold War are only beginning to seep out. Secret deals with Nazis and fascists, domestic spying and red-baiting, atomic radiation tests on military personnel and civilians, assassinations and the overthrow of third-world governments, plans for a first-strike nuclear attack — I will stop before I start sounding like Oliver Stone, producer of the film *JFK*. And yet, there remains the comment by a former US official that 'possibly, one-third of American history is classified.' Not to mention all the Official Secrets squirrelled away somewhere in Britain.

Moreover, perhaps no less so than in Japan, US history textbooks in the postwar decades excluded or limited reference to the darker events and persistent social struggles that had shaped US history and continued to do so. In favour of a Cold-War consensus and the pursuit of anti-Communism at home and abroad, high school history texts unanimously represented America's westward expansion and overseas interventions in terms of Manifest Destiny, the defence of the hemisphere and/or support of anti-colonial struggles. Naturally, democracy was a central theme of their narrative of progress; however, ignoring the persistent limitations, exclusions, oppressions and contradictions, these texts articulated, well before Fukuyama was old enough to think about it, a vision of a postwar liberal and capitalist USA as the culmination of western and world history.

Not only the schoolbooks, the most official of public histories, but all US mass culture from Madison Avenue to Hollywood projected that assumption. As the 1950s gave way to the 1960s, liberals and conservatives alike seemed to share in the historical belief that, aside from the continuing demands of the Cold War, in the US we were witness to the 'end of ideology'. Those who resisted were effectively marginalised and without credibility. Or so it seemed for a brief while...

Fomented in part by the very contradiction between the history portrayed and the history lived, yet at the same time part of a global democratic surge, US radicalism was renewed in the sixties; and the struggles for the civil rights of racial and ethnic minorities, the social rights of the poor, the equal rights of women and the cessation of imperial wars, along with the much less celebrated but no less remarkable working-class insurgencies demanding changes in industrial life, instigated serious reforms in US polity. These struggles also inspired dramatic revisions in historical study and thought, including the socialisation and democratisation of the past, the recovery and incorporation into the historical record of previously ignored class, racial and gender experiences and agencies.

Unfortunately, though predictably, these democratic campaigns and accomplishments also provoked profound reactions on the part of the 'power elite' who grew increasingly worried that the several struggles of the day were on the verge of coalescing into a broad radical-democratic movement promising reform on an even grander scale. In public statements and manifestos such as the Trilateral Commission's 1975 report, *The Crisis of Democracy*, the voices of the corporate class declaimed that the liberal polities were facing 'governmental overload', more specifically, a 'crisis' in which the problem of 'governance' stemmed from 'an excess of democracy'. The threat was clearly acknowledged as coming from below — from 'minorities, women, public-interest groups, white-collar unions' — but the real culprits were made out to be university and other 'value-oriented intellectuals' (for which, read historians and their kin).

Thus, for the past 20 years we have been subjected to vigorous and concerted campaigns to reshape historical memory, consciousness and imagination — the climax of which was to be the pronouncement that we had arrived at the 'end of history'.

Strongly encouraged and lucratively bankrolled by the business elites, in the course of the 1970s, Ronald Reagan and Margaret Thatcher along with their Republican and Conservative comrades brilliantly articulated mythical renditions of their respective nations' history which served at the outset to weld together their diverse New Right political alliances and, in time, to garner support for their electoral campaigns and subsequent endeavours domestic and foreign.

Gross distortions and occlusions of the past were incessant but, in particular, we might recall Reagan's harking back to a supposedly happier, safer and more economically robust USA existing some time — depending on your preferences and the occasion — before the upheavals and Great Society programmes of the 1960s or the New Deal of the 1930s. In Thatcher's historical memory, the good old days were those when 'Victorian Values' were supposed to have prevailed and the British people were somehow both more self-reliant and kinder and more entrepreneurial and philanthropic (the former or latter combination determined presumably by one's class circumstances).

Completely ignoring questions of exploitation and oppression, both

Reagan and Thatcher spoke of the past as a time of 'shared values' and insisted on the necessity of reinstating them. These were not flashes of nostalgia, but weapons directed against liberals, trade unionists, socialists, feminists, the poor, and racial and ethnic minorities. Each offered a rhetoric of consensus actually intended to bolster a politics of social division and a political economy of capital accumulation and class inequality.

The New Right leaders' ambitions for 'the past' were not merely rhetorical. Declaring in neo-McCarthyite language their hostility for the scholarly and pedagogical labours of the new critical historians, they initiated their 'culture wars' by translating the media-touted 'crisis of historical education' into a major civic, if not defence, issue. Then, under the guise of responding to student ignorance and spreading historical amnesia, Republican and Tory secretaries of education, respectively, introduced unprecedented schemes for 'national standards' and a 'national curriculum' in which history was to be a central subject. And they made every effort to determine that the narratives rendered in those syllabi and curricula would contribute to the development of their aspired-to conservative orders.

In this age of spectacle and entertainment, New Right efforts to subordinate historical education have been enhanced, if not overshadowed (at least in the US), by corporate, especially the corporate media's, reconstructions of history. In film, television, and advertising, past and present are sanitised and commodified; and now we have the proposal by the Disney Corporation to develop a new theme park, to be called 'Disney's America', that promises to create 'realistic renderings of the nation's past', including slavery and the Civil War. In a truly Orwellian fashion, we are to be provided history for the 'end of history'...

Just what is it about history that so distresses the ruling and governing classes that they are driven to control and command it? Inverting Orwell, Kundera writes: 'The past is full of life, eager to irritate us, provoke and insult us, tempt us to destroy or repaint it. The only reason people want to be masters of the future is to change the past. They are fighting for access to the laboratories where photographs are retouched and biographies and histories rewritten.' It is not confidence that authorises such actions, but trepidation; it is not conviction about the course of history which leads them to declare it finished, but anxiety induced by what they see there.

I began by proposing that we look directly into the eyes of the powerful, to discover what they see, what they recognise, what they know. I should have asked: what do they see, but try to obscure? What do they recognise, but attempt to deny? What do they know, but endeavour to conceal?

Russian socialist-democrat, Boris Kagarlitsky, refers us to Marx's own assessment of censorship: 'The law against a frame of mind is not a law of the state promulgated for its citizens but the law of one party against another party... Laws against frame of mind are the involuntary cry of a bad conscience.' Absolutely. But it is not only guilt that obliges proscriptions. Knowing this, Kagarlitsky adds the following: 'Censorship is introduced by those who fear public opinion, the very existence of censorship is a sign that oppositional thought is alive and cannot be eradicated — that alongside the ruling bureaucratic "party" there is also a de facto democratic party.'

Why do ruling classes fear history? Because, beyond their crimes, and beyond the tragedies and ironies which are so demanding of hope and spirit, they see and they know — as did their forerunners — that history has been, and remains, a process of struggle for freedom and for justice — and increasingly, at least since the late eighteenth century, it has been, as the late Raymond Williams once put it, a 'Long Revolution', at the political heart of which is the fight for liberty, equality and democracy.

Moreover, they realise that however many times history has entailed what Christopher Hill calls an 'experience of defeat', for the peoples and classes who have sought to make it otherwise, the Long Revolution has also afforded great victories. In search of reason to hope, Ronald Aronson ventures this: 'The real historical advances in human social morality have occurred through such struggles. Slavery has been abolished, democratic rights have been won, certain elements of dignity and equality promised and achieved, wars ended, other wars forestalled — only because we have acted. Projected now desperately, now with confidence, in collective visions by movement after movement, sacrificed for, agitated for, partially achieved, then legitimised by law and custom, social progress has been made true every step of the way.'

Indeed, it is not only the victories of resistance, rebellion and revolution that weigh in; the defeats, too, have contributed to the making of democracy. The Levellers and Diggers of seventeenth-century Albion and later generations of Radical, Luddite and Chartist artisans and

ASSOCIATED PRESS

Tiananmen Square, Beijing 1989: the face that launched 10,000 deaths

proletarians; the Parisian *sans-culottes* and Parisian communards; the rebellious black slaves of the Americas; the radical mechanics, Populist farmers, Socialist workers and Wobbly labourers, native and immigrant, of my own country; the revolutionary *campesinos, vaqueros* and *obreros* of Mexico; the workers defending Republican Spain and their comrades in the International Brigades; the partisans of occupied Europe and Jewish fighters in the Warsaw Ghetto; the anti-apartheid demonstrators at Sharpeville in South Africa; and the Chinese students and workers of 1919 and 1989, have all, in their respective ways, endowed the struggle.

The democratic narrative has long haunted the imagination of the powerful, and it must do so all the more today because it is the very foundation upon which contemporary political legitimacy stands. However insincere, hypocritical or blasphemous their words, for much of this century, and for far longer in the US, rulers and governors have been obliged to speak within, and to, a discourse of democracy — often, a discourse rooted in a revolutionary moment. However limited, debased or eviscerated the institutions, the idea of 'rule by the people' has become the ideological cornerstone of modern government...

Tormented by what they see in and know about the past and the making of the present, the powerful recognise, as Krushchev did, that, to the extent that they pursue their scholarly and pedagogical labours critically, historians can be 'dangerous people'. They are not only capable of wielding the powers of the past against the powerful themselves, but, by offering historical challenges to despair and cynicism, of making radical contributions to popular memory, consciousness and imagination.

Isaac Deutscher himself once wrote that the 'role of the intellectuals...is to remain eternal protestors.' I like that. However, in acknowledgement and appreciation of the fears of the powers that be, I would take it further — in a way I am sure he would have approved. Poaching a term from my mentor, Victor Kiernan, I would argue that our responsibility and task is to secure, bear witness to, and critically advance the *prophetic memory* of the struggle for democracy. Thus, for radical historians the fundamental project remains: the recovery of the past, the education of desire, and the cultivation, as Gramsci himself urged, of 'an historical, dialectical conception of the world which understands movement and change, which appreciates the sum of effort and sacrifice which the present has cost the past and which the future is costing the present, and which conceives the contemporary world as a synthesis of the past, of all past generations, which projects itself into the future.'

We cannot know what will transpire, but be assured that our governors fully expect the historic and perennial demand for power to the people to be renewed. It's reflected in their eyes. ❏

© Harvey Kaye
This essay is a shortened version of the 1994 Deutscher Memorial Lecture, the full text of which will appear in Harvey Kaye's forthcoming book, Why Do Ruling Classes Fear History? and Other Questions *(St Martin's Press/Macmillan)*

LETTER FROM GUJRANWALA

ALTAF GAUHAR

A short course in blasphemy

Even by its own standards, Pakistan is going through a turbulent phase of its brief history as obscurantist clerics fight would-be democrats for control of its future

Blasphemy is a subject with which I have a close personal connection. I was born in Gujranwala, the Pakistani city which recently hit the headlines of western newspapers, when two Christians were awarded the death penalty under the anti-blasphemy law. I loved the place as a child in the early 1920s for its milk and yoghurt and for its wrestlers, in particular Rahim 'pehlawan', who knocked out a British challenger, Hudson, in less than a minute. It was also the birthplace of the famous Sikh ruler, Raja Ranjit Singh. Several mosques and temples in the town served as centres of training for Hindu pundits and Muslim preachers.

The town had a large community of sweepers, all low-caste Hindus converted to Christianity by British missionaries during the Raj. Their principal occupation was to keep the town's open drains in as clean a state as possible — a pungent task which they could perform only when fortified by a heady local brew called *thurrah*. They were treated as 'untouchable' and members of other communities had no dealings with them. These Christians, once they were given enough money to acquire a large enough quantity of *thurrah* to inflame them, could also be used as agents by pundits and preachers to provoke communal disturbances. But more about that later.

Never a month passed, even in those days of highly disciplined British administration, when the town was not rocked by some communal incident resulting in rioting and arson. Now the Muslims would take to the streets shouting 'death to the Hindus' for planting a lump of pig flesh in the mosque, thus defiling its sanctity. In retaliation the Hindus would burn down some Muslim shops for throwing a large chunk of beef in a temple to compromise the chastity of *gaomata* (mother cow). The Christians, who consumed beef and bacon with equal relish, were the ones who were used for planting the offensive chunks of flesh in places of worship by rival Hindu and Muslim zealots. It was all a game of communal passion, played in the name of religion, in which innocent Christians were used as pawns, often with disastrous consequences.

The British penal code provided for stringent punishment for defiling a place of worship or imperilling the law and order situation by causing outrage to the religious beliefs of any community, but the punishment did not include the death penalty. The same provisions of law continued until Pakistan's third military ruler, General Zia ul Haq, embarked on what he called the process of Islamisation of laws. Blasphemy, by then, had become a matter of great concern for the religious parties in Pakistan. The Ahmadiya community had been expelled from the fold of Islam for their heretic beliefs though the Muslim divines could not agree on the definition of a true Muslim. The court of enquiry where this matter was considered observed: 'What is Islam and who is a 'Momin' or a Muslim? We put this question to the *ulema* (religious scholars) and we shall presently refer to their answers to this question. But we cannot refrain from saying here that it was a matter of infinite regret to us that the *ulema* whose first duty should be to have settled views on the subject, were hopelessly disagreed among themselves. Keeping in view the several definitions (of a Muslim) given by the *ulema,* need we make any comment except that no two learned divines are agreed on this fundamental? If we attempt our own definition as each learned divine has done, and that definition differs from that given by all others, we unanimously come out of the fold of Islam' (Justice Munir Enquiry Report, 1953).

The majority of the people of Pakistan are Sunni Muslims and the *ulema* who claim to represent them have always been agitating that the Shias, because of their blasphemous beliefs, pose a great threat to the integrity of Islam. To appease these *ulema* General Zia ul Haq amended the Penal Code to provide for the punishment of the offence of blasphemy in 1980. The amendment stated: 'Whoever by words, either

Lahore, Pakistan 1994: Manzoor Masih (near to camera) and Rehmat Masih behind bars

spoken or written, or by visible representation, or by any imputation, innuendo or insinuation, directly or indirectly defiles the sacred name of any wife, or members of the Holy Prophet, shall be punished with imprisonment of either description for a term which may extend to three years, or with fine, or with both.' The *ulema* were happy to have made their first major inroad into the judicial process though the lawyers were distressed by the extremely broad and vague formulation of the offence. The 'family' of the holy prophet was not defined nor was it indicated whether the word covered the descendants (which would include the Hashemite King Hassan of Jordan) up to the present times. Even a look of concern or a grin could be construed as a blasphemous insinuation. No particular procedure for the lodging of complaints and their investigation was prescribed. The assumption was that no Muslim would ever lodge a false complaint because such a complaint would constitute a blasphemous act.

It was all a game, played in the name of religion, in which Christians were used as pawns, often with disastrous consequences

Two years later the scope of the offence of blasphemy was widened when it was provided through an ordinance that 'Whoever wilfully defiles, damages or desecrates a copy of the holy Quran or an extract therefrom or uses it in any derogatory manner or for any unlawful purpose shall be punishable with imprisonment for life.' The first person to be punished for this offence was a Muslim preacher who had allegedly thrown a copy of the Quran in a pot of boiling milk in a fit of temper. The man was taken to the local police station but a crowd of angry believers dragged him out of the lock-up and lynched him — his body was later tied to the back of a motor cycle and dragged through the streets. Guess where the incident occurred? In the city of Gujranwala. Where else?

The religious groups had now acquired enough influence to compel General Zia to help them crush their sectarian rivals and other liberal groups who were agitating against the growth of a parallel legal system under the name of Islamisation. By now General Zia ul Haq had set up the Federal Shariat court which had been empowered not only to interpret but also expound the Islamic law. Their hope was that flogging, amputation of limbs and public hanging would soon become the accepted forms of punishment for a whole range of crimes. An article (295A) was added to the Pakistan Penal Code in 1986 which provided that: 'Whoever by words, either spoken or written, or by visible representation or by any imputation, innuendo, or insinuation, directly or indirectly, defiles the sacred name of the Holy Prophet Muhammad (peace be upon him) shall be punished with death or imprisonment for life and shall also be liable to fine.'

Gujranwala again! Three Christians belonging to different villages of Gujranwala, Salamat Masih, Rehmat Masih and Manzoor Masih were tried and sentenced to death by the trial court on 9 February 1995. The complaint was lodged by a certain Hafiz Fazle Haq, Imam of a mosque, in 1993 when Salamat Masih, one of the three accused, was only 12 years old. The Hafiz withdrew his complaint before the death sentence was pronounced but by then the court had come under the control of the crowd which would surround the courtroom during the hearing and demand the execution of the accused persons on the spot. The crowd was so enraged when the three Masihs were granted bail by the High Court of Lahore that one of them, Manzoor Masih, was shot dead outside the court building. The proceedings went on for two years because the prosecution could not produce any evidence to support the charge that the accused had been scribbling some scurrilous words derogatory to the holy prophet on the wall of the mosque, nor would they produce the chits of paper bearing the alleged blasphemous words which the accused had thrown into the compound of the mosque. The witnesses declined to repeat the objectionable words as the repetition would have amounted to a blasphemous act. It was pleaded on behalf of the defence that one of the accused was a minor and the other two were illiterate who could not have written the objectionable words. Despite the lack of any reliable evidence the trial court sentenced the accused persons to death.

The announcement of the sentence caused an outrage. The world press criticised Pakistan for sentencing two citizens to death under what was considered a 'barbaric' law. The prime minister of Pakistan, Benazir Bhutto, expressed 'shock' and most of the educated people in the country criticised the judgement which they knew had been passed under the pressure of certain religious groups whose supporters kept the court under siege throughout the trial of the case. An eminent jurist and a former chief justice of the High Court of Lahore, Dr Javed Iqbal, said

Pawns in the game of religion: Salamat Masih and relatives

that the blasphemy law, under which the trial had been held, was wholly inconsistent with the spirit of the Quranic injunctions on the subject. He maintained that nothing could be more blasphemous than denying the fact that Muhammad was a prophet of God and that the Quran was revealed to him. Since these two facts were implicitly or explicitly denied by the Jews, Christians and Hindus they should all be awarded the death penalty under the law of blasphemy. He argued persuasively that only a Muslim could be tried under the blasphemy law if he said or did anything derogatory to the prophet and the Quran. While the appeal was being heard in the High Court of Lahore, one of the religious leaders declared that if the appeal was allowed and the accused were set free he would himself strangle them to death. The attorney for the prosecution called the appeal court 'a kangaroo court' in which he had no confidence. Outside the court room the car of the defence attorney, Asma Jehangir, who had argued the case of the accused with singular courage, was smashed by a group of demonstrators. Some eminent lawyers who had been summoned to assist the court showed that the prosecution had failed to produce any evidence to justify the conviction of the accused. The court finally accepted the appeal and the accused persons were set free. The government knew that it could not guarantee their safety in freedom and they were soon despatched to Germany where they were granted political asylum.

These blasphemy cases demonstrate the state of law in Pakistan. The educated classes are deeply disturbed by the introduction of certain laws which they find alien to their culture. They are opposed to flogging and public hanging and that is the reason why General Zia's plan to introduce these punishments never succeeded. They find the law of blasphemy unacceptable because they do not recognise that the honour of the prophet and his family or the sanctity of the Quran is under threat in a country almost entirely populated by Muslims who deeply revere the prophet. They consider the sectarian controversies which have resulted in widespread violence wholly uncalled for. On the other hand there are the religious groups, none of whom has ever secured more than marginal support in the elections, who have turned the mosque into a platform of political agitation and who indulge in irresponsible rabble rousing in the name of Islam. They have acquired undue importance because successive military dictators have used them to consolidate their personal rule under the garb of Islam. As a result the cultural scene is dominated by a spirit of intolerance wholly alien to Islam or any democratic system of government. Fundamental human rights remain a vague and elusive concept: a believer invokes these rights in his own interest but rarely concedes them in the interest of any non-believer.

As a nation-state Pakistan is going through a turbulent phase of transition. What was conceived as a democratic polity is being converted into a theological state without any popular mandate. Undefined Islamic laws, wholly divorced from their social context, are being imposed on a society committed to adapting itself to the requirements of the modern age. This is being done by a small obscurantist group, divided into various sects, who are bent upon distorting the original vision of Pakistan as a democratic state in which every citizen will have equal rights, equal opportunities and equal status. They consider, as they had declared before Justice Munir's court of enquiry in 1953, that 'A state based on this idea is the creature of the devil.' ❏

Into the promised land

One year into its new age, South Africa has achieved much. Thanks to the overwhelming moral stature of Nelson Mandela, the worst has not happened, the best is to come. A report compiled by *Index*'s Africa editor, Adewale Maja-Pearce

Left: South Africa 1994: land of promises

Index *gratefully acknowledges the support of the Open Society for Adewale Maja-Pearce's work in South Africa*

ACHMAT DANGOR

Mama & Kid Freedom

Mama had them shot in the afternoon. They were lined up facing westwards, so that the only blindfold they would need was the glare of the sinking sun. And when the shooting stopped, their crumpled up bodies were dumped into heavy postal bags and dragged away. A Deputy President, a few Cabinet ministers, half a dozen Provincial Premiers. A secretary whose squint eyes Mama thought were an evil omen, was included at the last minute. Their blood did not have enough time to stain the earth.

Mama and Kid Freedom waited until the silence was absolute, then strode briskly towards the Cabinet Room where the rest were assembled. She walked ahead, the Kid a few paces behind, an unspoken order of precedence had quickly been established. They paused before the grief stricken portrait of the Old President, whose death a few weeks ago started all this. Kid stepped in front of her with a deftness that brought a smile to her face. He held open the door and stared at the dull faces seated around the table, until murmurs ceased and feet no longer shuffled and chairs stopped scraping, then stepped aside to let Mama in.

Nineteen days ago Mama sat up in bed in the middle of the night and said out loud 'he's dead.' She walked through the moonlit rooms of the villa throwing open doors and rousing her entourage in a loud and sonorous voice.

'The time has come, the time has come.'

The ones that were slow to respond, those making love and those who slept too deeply, the coldness of their guns held close to their hearts, were spurred on by kicks and the kind of abuse they had not heard from her tongue for a long time. Drowsy resignation — *it's just another of her crazy nights* — quickly turned to fearful wakefulness. There was a demonic brightness in her, recognised especially by the older hands. Many were certain that her eyes were closed, as if she herself was in a deep sleep, even when she gave the most detailed instruction for their departure, repeating over and over again, 'The time has come.'

Her emissaries worked the phones throughout the night and the next day, until Mama was ready to leave her 'prison' at the mouth of the Umtata River, surrounded by walls of sea and the cloistered comfort of wind-bent trees. She sat swaying in the look-out seat of an armoured car as they drove along the stony road to the city of Umtata, followed by a unit of serious young men, their naked chests gilded by dust and manly sweat.

The ascetic column, Mama at its stoic head, soon swelled into a caravanserai of singing men and dancing women. In each village that they passed, there were people who knew that they wanted to be part of this deadly column. They had not seen so much theatre since the days when the Old President was a younger man. Anything was better than the dull virtue of patience and restraint he had asked them to suffer. Many did not even know who Mama was, though they heard vague legends of a famous witch who came to seek refuge from the righteousness of the city people up North. Nor did they really appreciate the solemn nature of half-mast flags when eventually they streamed onto the tarmac at Umtata Airport. People could not understand why no-one joined in their festive chants and refused to dance the rhythmic freedom dance that everyone knew so well. Even Mama, the woman who sat without stirring on the swaying seat for two days on end, now wept as she alighted, and embraced those who came to greet her.

Only Kid Freedom Mhlangu as he was simply known then, recognised the sense of occasion that the simple villagers had anticipated, the pomp and circumstance that they had marched so far to experience. He rose from the bowels of the troop carrier where he and other of Mama's advisors were seated throughout the journey, intoxicated by the petrol fumes and dirt they had inhaled, and climbed up to Mama's vacant seat. Despite her angry glances, he began to cheer.

'Viva Mama, Viva Freedom, Kill the faggots, kill the whores!' he screamed and began to dance, a long forgotten *toyi-toyi*[1] of stamping feet and roughly swaying shoulders. The crowd drowned out his voice with the roar of their own response, but his words were of little consequence. What mattered was the poetry of the chant, the musicality of his military march upon the precarious stage of a wobbly look-out seat. He finished with a rousing 'Viva Mama, Viva Freedom.'

Mama smiled and announced that Kid Freedom, as he would henceforth be known, was to be her General, then climbed up the stairway to an enormous airplane, turning to wave at the multitude, who cheered even though they saw how closely she was followed by a gang of disaffected politicians, deposed tribal despots and unfrocked generals. Those familiar slanted faces brought only a momentary pause to the ancient ululations of praise. People sensed that they had been close to history that day. This, their parents told them, was the way life was when the Old President was first released from prison. Anyway, they had not had so much fun for a long time.

'There is my mandate!' Mama told her critics and waved her hands at the giant TV screens which showed, over and over, the scenes of wild jubilation at Umtata Airport. This is a good story, journalists said. They had not had such good stories for a long time, except for the President's death. And you can only do so much with the solemnities of a funeral. He was good man, but dull in his last days and quite autocratic. He allowed none of this riotous venting of emotions, the smashing of shop windows, the burning of the flags of unity.

'Our people want a strong leader,' Mama said.

'A breath of fresh air,' Kid Freedom added.

On a night wild with the smell of rain, they began by rounding up the gays. Cars, trucks, vans, jeeps, seven Cadillacs bought on a junket to

Detroit and marooned by the Old President's rage were pressed into service. Any vehicle that the Security Forces could muster. People were picked up in bars and cafes, snatched from sidewalks where men and women foolishly felt free to stroll in the warm Spring air despite the talk of a coup. Others were taken from their homes, their heads covered with hoods. 'You never know who's homo,' a spokesman said. 'It is to free us of this vermin.'

When that suddenly familiar fanfare of crashing car doors and screaming tyres was over, a silence fell over the streets. The gays were gone and the rest had fled indoors. In darkened homes mothers counted the silhouette of heads, acknowledging with startled cries the absence of a son or daughter or husband. People took to speaking in whispers and homespun codes, finding names for police and politicians, for jails and death, for the migratory birds who were their children or wives or husbands or lovers on the run. Just like the old days before the Old Man came out of prison.

Don't worry, *Ingolovane*[2] will get them, Mama and her kind, someone said.

Kid Freedom sat in his office on Hero's Heights, comforted by the chatter in the Command Room alongside. Numbers were being totted up, the capacity of jails and detention centres calculated. Someone suggested re-opening Robben Island.

The whole Cape Peninsular is full of fucking *moffies*[3]. The jails are full!

'Hey, the Kid's listening,' a voice said.

The door shut, leaving Kid by himself. Being alone made him feel uneasy, as if there was another person in the room. He had to shrug this off. Paranoia. The stress, the responsibility. He looked around the office, walls stripped of photographs and decorations, the polished desk with its neat stacks of Top Secret files, carpetless floors, a spartan soldierliness that filled him with pride. He had come a long way, delinquent and renegade to General of the Security Forces. Today they had disposed of some of the old leadership, the rebellious ones, the ones whose faces were known, the ones whose eyes betrayed their dislike of Mama even while they smiled, dispatched without ceremony, a fitting end! And still the gays are being rounded up. How many are there?

He reached into his drawer and removed a bottle of brandy, a brand no longer seen in the country. Everything was for export, earn foreign exchange. That's what they did to this country. A soldier burst through the door. Kid Freedom's rare moment of savoured solitude shattered.

'General, Mama's here, I mean the President.'

Mama stood in the doorway, her hair freed from the prison of her famous headscarf stood wildly on end, a bright shawl held tightly to her near-naked body. She had the sleepy look of an innocent child. No-one must see her like this. The soldier had already retreated into the Command Room's bustle.

'Find him!'

'Who?'

'*Ingolovane*! Find him.'

Kid Freedom saw for the first time that her eyes were closed, that she navigated the darkness of her eyelids with the antenna of an outstretched hand, as she spun around and left him in the cold austerity of his office. All around the country Security Forces were placed on alert.

'Find him,' Kid Freedom commanded, 'Find Siphiso *Ingolovane*.'

'It doesn't make sense General,' an officer protested, '*Ingolovane* is not even a name.'

'Mama has sensed him, he exists. Find him, or there will be no peace in this country,' Kid Freedom answered tersely.

They began the search on the mines, among the miners asleep in their compounds, for *Ingolovane*, they heard, was a carrier-of-gold. And followed his trail to his family in the villages, where it was possible for him to hide, for these carriers of ore were a clannish lot who quickly forgot the distinction between right and wrong and whose only loyalty was to each other. An intelligence source said he could be gay, what with a name like that, or an actor or a writer. The net widened, until the jails were too full and detainees walked free because the guards could not cope and the cities were pock-marked by darkened windows and drawn shutters. Until the soldiers were edgy from lack of sleep and shot at shadows in the street.

Ingolovane's name was the same in Zulu and Sotho, though no-one knew whether Siphiso was the name his father gave him, since Mama's Zulu ally denied that the man was of his tribe. Informers reported seeing him in different guises in a dozen places at the same time. He was a ganja-smoking dreadlocked youth, a businessman whose suit pockets were stuffed with contraband dollars, a woman — a whore — dressed as a man, a spirit of darkness who threw outlawed bones to determine the future. No-one, it seemed, had ever looked into his eyes and said he had no eyes but hollowed out cavities in his skull.

When they switched on their TV sets, not to watch *Loving*, which Mama, bless her soul, had reintroduced, but to hear the latest news about the rebel and murderer Siphiso *Ingolovane*, the son of a Hillbrow[4] prostitute and drunken migrant worker, they saw Mama's face, no longer warm and smiling and motherly as their own, her long-suffering quietness had given way to a brooding anger, while others spoke, that young man in particular, the one with the strange name, Kid Freedom. Which mother would give her child a name like that? He's not someone you can trust.

When Mama announced that they had caught this mister *Ingolovane* and had to shoot him, the rabid dog that he was, and burn his bones to prevent contamination of the air that good people breathed, everyone laughed. They had heard, on good authority, that Mama herself was hiding him, captivated by his beauty, she was keeping him all to herself. Bad blood was growing between Mama and Kid Freedom, that the charlatan kings and bitter politicians were returning to their mountain hideaways, that Mama had imported a thousand new wigs.

Somewhere in a city street a man sat down beneath a coloured awning. No, he said, he was not *Ingolovane* come back from the dead. He wanted a coffee, milk without sugar. He was sick and tired of those soaps. Hollywood crap. ❏

Notes: 1. A military step developed by guerrilla soldiers and which has evolved into a popular rhythmic prance 2. A word of Zulu origins to describe both the process and the cart used to transport gold ore from underground to the surface. The word was adopted by most speakers of indigenous languages. 3. A (often derogatory) word to describe gay men 4. A 'sleazy' part of Johannesburg

NADINE GORDIMER

ISOLDE OHLBAUM/BLOOMSBURY

Act two: one year later

1. Accept nothing as true which I did not clearly recognise to be so; that is to say, to avoid carefully precipitation and prejudice, and to accept nothing in my judgments beyond what presented itself so clearly and distinctly to my mind, that I should have no occasion to doubt it.
2. Divide each of the difficulties which I examined into as many parts as possible, and might be necessary in order best to resolve them.
3. Carry on my reflections in order, starting with those objects that were most simple and easy to understand, so as to rise little by little, by degrees, to the knowledge of the most complex: assuming an order among those that did not naturally fall into a series.
4. Last in all cases, make enumerations so complete and reviews so general that I should be sure of leaving nothing out. (Descartes)

May I be at all sure that I can follow Descartes' method when gathering together this single year that has taken up within its unique newness, its surge to the future, all that was held back, accumulated in the conflicting stalemates of the past? It's a toppling wave; 12 months is hardly enough time to regain breath. I'll have a go.

Best to begin with Rule 3. Indeed, the order of reflection cannot be chronological, but rises to mind idiosyncratically, the public events see-sawing with the private ones, and so the personal value system has to be sorted out from the politico-social one. It is simple and easy to understand my own sense of joy when, again and again, I've seen friends whom I've known as exiles, prisoners, outcasts, hunted occupants of the underground, now bearing high office and deferred to by international dignitaries, their formerly banned voices quoted in the press and their forbidden faces blooming on the TV screen.

Jessie Duarte, who lived up to her image as a diminutive firebrand, when, in detention a few years ago, she led the women to burn their mattresses in protest at their imprisonment without trial: this year, as Gauteng minister of safety and security, she's sturdily on the other side of the legal dispensation, facing taxi warmen and police on strike, and in February elegantly followed protocol when introducing the Queen of England at an official lunch. Albie Sachs, half an arm and one eye blown away by a hit squad of the apartheid government; now sitting as a judge in the Constitutional Court. Mongane Wally Serote, poet in exile working for the ANC around the world, now taking his seat as a duly elected member of parliament. To measure up to Rule 1: I accept as true, and clearly recognise to be so, that justice has come about in the persons of these individuals, and justice is sweeter to see than revenge.

On to the most complex of what has happened. The general public events. It would take more pages than my quote to divide (Rule 2) each of the difficulties I ought to examine — or rather my own reaction to them — and to resolve all within myself. A series: the shambling off the scene of the white right-wing extremists whom I feared, last year; by contrast, the continuing petulant troublemaking of Buthelezi that was to be expected; and the unexpected dangers of Winnie Mandela's will to power. To turn back the clock is not something I should ever wish to do, from our present, with the exception in respect of Winnie Mandela. I wish we could re-run her emergence, hand in hand with Nelson Mandela, from his prison, so that this extraordinary woman, whom I have known and warmly respected through many early years, could see that if she had kept her place beside him she would have been no mere consort. He is the greatest statesman and leader in the world today — a fulfilment of everything we could have hoped for on the 27 April last year. The couple would have doubled the impact, a unique combination in that world and our part of it. *That* was where her power lay.

Another difficulty to be faced clearly and distinctly in my mind is what is known as labour unrest. Strikes are represented in the press at home and abroad as the sure sign that things are going wrong in our country; overseas investors withdraw their heads into their corporate shells.

A failure of democracy that workers go on strike?

What do we want — the 'industrial peace' of our old police state?

Only those brave or foolhardy enough among workers dared to strike then. Teargas, dogs and guns were the form of negotiation offered them. The strikes are a proof that democracy is coming into practice in our country. Painfully, yes. What 'goes wrong' with these industrial actions is one of the heritages of apartheid that will continue to plague us for a long time. While rightfully taking up demands for a living wage (I've just heard that the lowest-ranking constable in our police force is supposed to live on R700 [US$192] a month), safe working conditions in mines and factories, a say in management, and the opening of a company's books to scrutiny, the trade unions have not yet educated their members on the relation between production, profits, and earnings. And the bosses have not wished to educate themselves on the relation between workers and bosses in a democracy; after decades when all you had to do was bring in a load of migratory workers and set them before the right levers and switches, like Chaplin in *Modern Times*, the men in the boardroom find it difficult to understand that in a democracy there can be industrial peace only if the workers are represented not by proxy or tokenism but in person, in policy-making and management decisions. That's the kind of modern times needed, for our place and era.

'Workers shall have the right to form and join trade unions...

Workers and employers shall have the right to organise and bargain collectively'

Interim Constitution

Some of what were apprehensively anticipated to be the most complex (Rule 3 again) in the series of events in our first year have happily disproved fear, for me. The opening of the 1995 school year in January was one such. Here was transformation of our world beginning at the *real beginning*: with children. Large numbers of black children — both those who live with their parents in the city as part of the exodus from segregated townships, and those whose parents brought them that morning from segregated townships to suburban schools — were registered at what had been white schools. It wasn't necessary to have these children escorted by police or army, as happened when schools were desegregated in the USA. There occurred less than a handful of

Soweto 1995: the first stage in unlearning apartheid

incidents where white people gathered in protest. Of course, the majority of black children in the urban and rural ghettos apartheid created are still without enough schools or teachers — a vast lack. But each time, at the end of a school day, I pass and see black and white children streaming out of class, the small boys scuffling joyfully, the girls giggling together, I know that something at the very base of our lives has changed from the shameful to the genesis of human fulfilment.

The injunction (Rule 4) to be sure to leave nothing out?

I could not attempt to follow that because, in the period of a single year, so much remains to be addressed, so much has had to be 'left out', for another year; years. For myself, I may have been troubled by some turns of events, but I have been neither disappointed nor disillusioned; it's been a year of awesome achievement, set against what preceded it for generations.

To maintain a healthy balance, of course, I quote Leibniz's gibe that Descartes' rules were 'like the precepts of some chemist; take what you need and do what you should, and you will get what you want..'

Well, I continue to believe it shall be so. ❏

© Nadine Gordimer

Code of conduct for schools (Congress of South African Students — COSAS)

The situation in our schools has dropped to an all-time low when it comes to effective learning and teaching. The culture of respect for adults and learning has been thrown away. All this is done under the pretext of being engaged in the struggle for a better education.

Our perspective and attitude is that the struggle for education and economic growth needs to be waged in a principled and disciplined manner for us to achieve our goal. The call made by the democratic forces for the ending of apartheid structures, does not imply that our schools should not have rules or a code of conduct. It is, therefore, according to this understanding that alternative structures such as PTSAs [Parent Teacher Student Associations] and SRCs [Student Representative Councils] have been developed.

This document will therefore seek to address the situation and behaviour of both teachers and students in schools. In so doing, we wish to establish values and standards in line with our major goal in education: to create a non-racial, democratic, and dynamic education — an education that will train us to be responsible parents and members of society. This document will also seek to protect the rights of students and teachers, the aim of which is to create a harmonious, mutual and humble relationship between teachers and students. This is a situation where co-operation and trust should prevail between students, teachers and parents. Therefore, in the process of implementing the disciplinary measures mentioned below, caution needs to be taken and punishment needs to be applied in accordance with the offence committed by an individual....

Pledge of support

I pledge my support for the detailed COSAS code of conduct for schools.
I am committed to the development of the full potential of myself and all other students and teachers.
I dissociate myself from all forms of violence, vandalism and other inappropriate conduct in our schools, colleges and universities, acknowledging that our struggle is now one to get educated and help make the South African economy grow.
I commit myself to
• look after and protect schools and school property
• support and be subject to appropriate and fair school discipline and due criminal process by the courts
• be punctual for school
• be respectful in dealings with teachers and students
• do homework, classwork, tests and other academic tasks
• help, where I can, in the renovation and upkeep of my school.
I undertake not to
• destroy or steal school books
• bully or victimise teachers and students
• smoke drugs or bring alcohol to school
• bring weapons to school or anything else that may endanger the lives of students and teachers

Signature .... ❏

ADEWALE MAJA-PEARCE

Welcome to the new South Africa

If the turmoil in the universities is anything to go by, there are no grounds for optimism says a visitor

How does one write about South Africa, one year after the demise of apartheid, without dragging in the whole tiresome business of colour that was supposed to have been jettisoned under the new dispensation? Over lunch in the Senior Common Room at Johannesburg's University of the Witwatersrand, for instance, I couldn't help noticing that the overwhelming majority of the dons were white and that the staff who served them were black. In other words, this microcosm of South African society — whites at the top; blacks at the bottom; the in-betweens only faintly glimpsed here and there — looked much like it did in the bad old days, but then what did I expect? One year was hardly long enough to produce the trained personnel who would guarantee what might be considered a fairer balance between what used to be known as the 'races', but even to put it this way is itself suspect since it partakes of the language that underpinned the injustice in the first place. Whites were no less South African because they were white, except that the matter could hardly be so simple for the previously disenfranchised who continued to find themselves in much the same position they were in before they went to the polls to elect a majority government. Colour may indeed have been rendered a political irrelevancy, in short, but it still remained a social fact, as witness the recent upheavals within the university itself.

Outside the cosy atmosphere of the Senior Common Room, where excellent Cape wines are sold at subsidised prices and the menu is calculated to satisfy all but the most demanding of palates, black students have been involved in a series of ongoing protests since last October. The

CARLOS REYES/ANDES PRESS AGENCY

Witwatersrand University, Johannesburg 1994: commitment to change?

initial pretext was the dismissal of two cashiers on allegations of theft. This quickly led to a hostage drama involving staff and students that resulted in the dismissal of nine other workers, disciplinary action against a further 39, and the suspension of 11 students; but the deeper problem, according to the students themselves, was the inability or the unwillingness of the university governing council to reconstitute itself according to the new political reality. Power still remains, as it has always done, in the hands of whites, almost invariably male; the students, for their part, are demanding the 'Africanisation' of the council, ie the presence of more black faces, as proof that the authorities are serious about their commitment to the changed times.

'Every person shall have the right to respect for, and protection of, his or her dignity'

Interim Constitution

The problem is not unique to the University of the Witwatersrand. At the Soweto, Sebokeng, Bloemfontein and Port Elizabeth campuses of

Vista University, for instance, black students are also demanding the resignation of the mainly white councils. To this end, they have embarked on a boycott of classes until the authorities accede to their demands, which also include student representation at departmental meetings where academic policy is formulated, and participation in the development of new curricula. At yet another tertiary institution, the Technikon Orange Free State, matters reached a head in March this year when security guards fired bird-shot at protesting students who were attempting to force their way into the student bureau to demand the resignation of the director. Eleven students were wounded, two of them seriously.

Given the enormous challenges facing the new South Africa, the problems currently besetting the tertiary institutions would seem to be relatively insignificant within the context of the wider society. In fact this is not so, unless one insists on taking the students' demands purely at their face value, which is the mistake that the authorities themselves appear to have made, hence the current stalemate. The governing council of the University of Vista's Soweto campus, for instance, was quick to point out that one of their number, Fikile Bam, is not only black but actually served time with Nelson Mandela on Robben Island. The implication, of course, is that Fikile Bam's presence among them constitutes irrefutable evidence of 'progress', not to say good faith, the corollary being that the students' refusal to grasp the revolutionary nature of the changes which have actually taken place merely betrays the level of their political immaturity: Look, they say (or, rather, don't quite say, but let that pass for the moment), not only black but...a former political prisoner.

That the white council members themselves fail to understand why such apparent radicalism may not seem so radical to those who know perfectly well why Robben Island existed in the first place and why it

'Every person shall have the right to freedom of movement anywhere within the national territory'

'Every citizen shall have the right freely to choose his or her place of residence anywhere in the national territory'

Interim Constitution

survived for so long is a measure of the gulf that separates the opposing camps. And having established the moral high ground, to their own satisfaction if no-one else's, the way is then left clear for the authorities to point out that, after all, they derived their positions according to the terms of both the South African Constitution and the University Act, such recourse to the strict letter of the law, a familiar enough refuge under the old order, being only marginally less dishonest than the argument that to accede to the students' demands will set a bad precedent and must therefore be countered on that score alone.

'Every person or community dispossessed of rights in land before the commencement of this Constitution...shall be entitled to claim restitution of such rights subject to and in accordance with sections...'

Interim Constitution

As in the universities, so in the society at large. It's perfectly true that blacks can live anywhere they please, just as it's perfectly true that some blacks — Cabinet ministers, say, and those fortunate enough to have been co-opted onto the boards of multinationals — have acquired mansions in the exclusive suburbs of Johannesburg and Pretoria and Cape Town, but the continued existence of the *structures* which ensure that most blacks continue to live in the townships because they can't afford to live anywhere else is hardly answered by pointing to the guarantees contained in the new constitution. On the contrary, the recourse to such legalism could only be calculated to set the townships aflame, which is why the politicians, but especially the white politicians, are rather more circumspect in their responses to demands for fundamental change than are their counterparts on the university councils.

And structures in the wider sense than might be supposed by the otherwise radical change in the country's political landscape from a closed, authoritarian society to an open, democratic one in which everybody is free to go where they please and live where they want, at least in theory. In practice, however, nobody outside the 'extremist' and therefore misguided minority groups is seriously proposing the wholesale redistribution of wealth on the grounds that the system which the previously Communist ANC inherited is fundamentally unjust, which also raises the suspicion that the ANC was only able to achieve power when the beneficiaries of the old order were satisfied that their inherited privileges would continue to be guaranteed. In any case, one only has to look at the mess which the rest of the continent has made of its liberation to caution against the excesses which would turn South Africa into yet another African basket-case.

'Every person shall have the right to his or her personal privacy, which shall include the right not to be subject to searches of his or her person, home or property, the seizure of private possessions or the violation of private communications'

Interim Constitution

There are probably as many commentators as there are ideas to explain Africa's failure to enter into a modern relationship with the century more than 30 years after independence; but the average South African (black, white or in-between) contemplating the bleak immensity north of the Limpopo river is bound to wonder whether it isn't better to just leave things as they are because, after all, the country at least works, proof of which is the number of economic refugees ready to scrub floors and work in the mines. 'Why is it that the black man messes everything up?' a coloured taxi driver asked me as he drove me to the airport to catch my flight back to Nigeria, where the military government was busy imprisoning all those who dared to doubt its legitimacy. It took a coloured to say what was on (almost) everybody's mind precisely because he was a coloured, which is to say neither black nor white at the same time as he partook of both, and to do so without any particular agenda. Five minutes later, while I was still if-ing and but-ing and sounding desperately unconvincing even to my own ears, he hooted at a black man in another car which pulled up alongside us. 'My friend,' he said, with genuine pleasure. It turned out that they went fishing together every weekend.

As regards the continuing upheavals in the universities, it would have been more truthful for the council members to come out and say that what they were really afraid of was the erosion of standards that is everywhere else the legacy of 'Africanisation', but of course they could hardly admit as much, except perhaps in private. The students themselves know this well enough but are equally discomfited by its implications, which is precisely why they continue to goad the authorities, and why, ultimately, the problem is proving so intractable. And if the universities are indeed a microcosm of the larger society, one hardly needs a crystal ball to be pessimistic concerning the country's future. Welcome to the new South Africa. ❏

Political violence March 1995

Eighty-five people died in political violence in March, the lowest death toll since the Human Rights Committee of South Africa started to monitor the situation in July 1990. It also marks a significant drop on the monthly average for the year to date — 115.6 — itself half the 236.5 in 1994. Deaths for 1995 total 347.

Regionally, Gauteng — East and West Rand, including Pretoria, Johannesburg and Soweto — bucked the national trend with 16 deaths compared to last month's six. The increase was largely the result of industrial conflict in the mines and the continuing 'taxi wars' between rival operators in Soweto. Together these accounted for 15 of the deaths.

While violence between rival political parties in Kwazulu-Natal dropped to its lowest level since October 1994, the province continues to have the worst record: 57 died in March, mainly in clashes between Mangosuthu Buthelezi's Inkatha Freedom Party and the African National Congress, compared to 76 the previous month. By and large, violence between party supporters in the workers' hostels has calmed down.

At 151 for the month, injuries from violence in March showed no similar decrease. However, the 1995 monthly average of 119.6 was a healthy drop on the figure for 1994, 244.6. ❏ *Source:* Monthly Report *of the HRCSA*

• *The latest report on human rights violations examines the record of the South African Police (SAP) before and after the April elections. Breaking with the past? Reports of alleged human rights violations by the South African Police, published on 7 May and compiled by the Network of Independent Monitors, the Trauma Centre for Victims of Violence and Torture, and the Independent Board of Inquiry, claims that the police are still involved in torture, assaults and unlawful shootings. A year after the election, it concludes, 'Continued human rights violations are the single greatest threat to the successful transformation of the old SAP.'*

GUY BERGER

New barons of the press

The ownership of South Africa's press is changing fast. Alternative papers are vanishing, foreigners moving in, and new monopolies are being formed

The old white-dominated set-up used to come under fire for the influence of its owners on editorial content, and for being part of a monopolistic media system that marginalised black South Africans as owners, journalists and readers. The exception was the alternative press with its own distinctive pattern of ownership and editorial.

Now, however, there are unpredicted developments in a media situation that two years ago looked as though nothing would ever shift. In terms of ownership (and a whole lot more), a great deal is happening in both mainstream and alternative sectors. Most noticeable has been a major collapse in the once vibrant alternative sector since the unbanning of the ANC in 1990, when the old white mainstream press began to encroach on 'alternative press' turf: black politics, human rights abuses, even investigative and educational journalism.

The circulations of the alternatives had always been tiny, but their influence, and their congruence with the mass of South Africans, had led them to believe they were destined to be the new mainstream in the new order. Having survived years under a state of emergency, they succumbed after liberation to the commercial realities of South Africa's skewed market-place.

Democracy did not touch the pricey printing and distribution systems sewn up by the mainstream, nor the needs of advertisers interested only in the number of readers per rand. Without the crutch of foreign funding (which ran dry in proportion to South Africa 'normalising'), it was an unequal contest and the alternatives lost hands down to the mainstream.

There was a momentary glimmer of hope when the mainstream owners agreed in 1993 to set up the Independent Media Diversity Trust, with a view to channelling new funds to the alternatives. The reason for their magnanimity was partly political pressure from the ANC and partly pressure from world newspaper owners grouped in FIEJ, the International Federation of Newspaper Publishers. A precondition for mainstream accession to FIEJ membership was the formation of a unified print industry in South Africa. The alternative weeklies agreed to unite with the mainstream in the Newspaper Press Union on condition of mainstream money for the IMDT.

But two years later, and at a time when ANC pressure on press ownership has evaporated under the change of events (see below), mainstream donations to the IMDT have all but ceased. The trust never really got the cash or the management expertise to save either the alternative press or the host of smaller community successors started in the 1990s. By April 1995, South Africa had lost *New Era* magazine, *Grassroots*, *Work in Progress*, *New African*, *Vrye Weekblad*, *South*, *Speak*, *Learn and Teach* and the *Eagle*, *Saamstaan* and *NamakwaNuus* had suspended publication. *Weekly Mail* survives through a partnership with the *Guardian* (UK), and *New Nation* was bought out by the mainstream.

This mainstream itself is also in major flux. Its changes in ownership date back to 1992. At the time, the ANC planned to establish its own daily paper, and espoused strong intentions of legislating an unbundling of press concentration. An ANC media charter that year called for the 'equitable redistribution' of media resources, and a need to 'ensure a diversity of ownership of media production and distribution facilities.'

These developments spurred Anglo American Corporation, which through Johannesburg Consolidated Investments (JCI) is the ultimate owner of the white English-language press, into taking the strategic decision to divest itself of what was proving to be an asset that was 'far removed from their core business but one with the most nuisance value'.

This move effectively pre-empted the ANC's slow-moving bid for its own paper — and took the sting out of criticism of media concentration. Argus went on sale in 1994 and Irish newspaper magnate, Tony O'Reilly, said to be a friend of Nelson Mandela's, scooped the entire Argus company at what one magazine described as 'a ridiculously low price'. The deal secured him *The Star, Daily News, Pretoria News, Diamond Field*

South African press in black and white

Advertiser, Sunday Tribune, the Newspaper Printing Company (which prints Argus and Times Media Limited (TML) papers in Johannesburg), and Allied Publishing (which distributes Argus and TML papers throughout the country).

This was something new on the South African scene: no newspaper

up to this point had really been identified with an individual owner —
not even with Harry Oppenheimer, despite his name being synonymous
with Anglo American.

The purchase broke up Anglo American's print empire, leaving the
corporation with TML, owned mainly through a consolidated Argus
Holdings renamed Omnimedia. It held the titles of the *Sunday Times,*
Business Day and the *Financial Mail*. In Port
Elizabeth, it retained its monopoly on the
English-language dailies with *Eastern Province*
Herald and the *Evening Post*.

TML's other titles were speedily bought up
by O'Reilly. He acquired in Cape Town the
Cape Times (where he already had the *Argus*),
and in Durban, the *Natal Mercury* (where he
already had the *Daily News)*. Argus also
bought out TML's 45 per cent stake in the
Pretoria News, which, with the *Diamond Field*
Advertiser, gave it a monopoly on English-
language dailies in four cities. Today, Tony
O'Reilly holds 50 per cent of the total
market, and 72 per cent of English-language
papers.

> 'All media financed by or
> under the control of the
> state shall be regulated
> in a manner which
> ensures impartiality and
> the expression of a
> diversity of opinion'
>
> *Interim Constitution*

The TML buy-out was controversial in Cape
Town, with a consortium of local black business calling on the
Competition Board to halt the sale so that they could put in a bid.
O'Reilly was urged not to buy the *Cape Times*, and TML was asked to
consider selling to the consortium. But the sale went ahead, with
agreement to appoint independent and non-executive directors onto the
regional board.

The new Argus owner launched a national business paper inserted in
all Argus papers except the part-owned *Sowetan*. In consequence, business
people, already served by TML's *Business Day*, and three weekly specialist
magazines, are being spoilt for choice.

Thanks to Tony O'Reilly, South Africa's media received an inflow of
foreign investment and an injection of competition. However, probably
for financial reasons, the new-found rivalry between Argus and other
press players has not seen any servicing of the lower end of the media
market where the majority of South African readers are located.

'INDEX *has bylines that Vanity Fair would kill for. Would that bylines were the only things about* INDEX *people were willing to kill for.*'

—Boston Globe

United Kingdom & Overseas (excluding USA & Canada)

	UK:	Overseas:	Students: £25
1 year—6 issues	£32	£38	
2 years—12 issues	£59	£70	
3 years—18 issues	£85	£105	

Name

Address

Postcode

£ _____ total.

❑ Cheque (£) ❑ Visa/Mastercard ❑ Am Ex ❑ Diners Club

Card No.

Expiry   Signature   B5A3

❑ I would also like to send **INDEX** to a reader in the developing world—just £22. These sponsored subscriptions promote free speech around the world for only the cost of printing and postage.

Return to: INDEX, Freepost, 33 Islington High Street, London N1 9BR
Telephone: 0171 278 2313 **Facsimile:** 0171 278 1878

United States and Canada

	US$:	Students: $35
1 year—6 issues	$48	
2 years—12 issues	$90	
3 years—18 issues	$136	

Name

Address

Postcode

$ _____ total.

❑ Cheque (US$) ❑ Visa/Mastercard ❑ Am Ex ❑ Diners Club

Card No.

Expiry   Signature   B5B3

❑ I would also like to send **INDEX** to a reader in the developing world—just $33. These sponsored subscriptions promote free speech around the world for only the cost of printing and postage.

INDEX
ON CENSORSHIP

33 Islington High Street, London N1 9LH England Facsimile: 0171 278 2313

INDEX ON CENSORSHIP
33 Islington High Street
London N1 9BR
United Kingdom

BUSINESS REPLY MAIL

FIRST CLASS PERMIT NO.7796 NEW YORK, NY

Postage will be paid by addressee.

INDEX ON CENSORSHIP
c/o Fund for Free Expression
485 Fifth Avenue
NEW YORK, NY   10164-0709

If not as owners or readers, black South Africans have benefited from the O'Reilly arrangements in editorial representation. The new boss has instituted a programme of affirmative action among journalists, and appointed the first black editor of a white newspaper, Moegsien Williams, formerly editor of *South*, who now runs the *Pretoria News*.

Fears were expressed about the Argus buy-out that despite O'Reilly's assurances of editorial independence, his newspapers would henceforth be accountable not to a board of directors, but to a strong-willed individual friendly with the state president.

So far, political interference has not materialised. But there certainly is commercial involvement in editorial under the new regime. All Argus editors now have to report to a regional manager with a strong business orientation — the upshot of which was the principled resignation of respected editor of *The Star*, Richard Steyn, in early 1995. The growing commercialisation of the press is a spectre looming large in South Africa.

Concerns about media barons and their involvement in editorial arose not only with Tony O'Reilly's entry into the media market. They were also present when black entrepreneur and ANC supporter Dr Nthatho Motlana took a majority share in the pro-Azapo/PAC *Sowetan*, owned up till then by Argus. 'We were hit by a double whammy — sold first to Tony O'Reilly and then to Dr Motlana,' quipped *Sowetan* editor Aggrey Klaaste.

The *Sowetan* deal represents another new factor in the pattern of South African newspaper ownership. Through his Johannesburg Stock Exchange (JSE) listed company, Motlana has now set out to build a black South African media empire, and has concluded a successful deal with alternative paper *New Nation*, which had unsuccessfully sought salvation for a long while with TML. As a result, the country's biggest daily, as well as an influential weekly, are today owned, if not wholly independently, by black South Africans, staffed (at most levels) by black South Africans, and targeted at black South Africans.

To date, fears of political interference have failed to materialise: like O'Reilly, Motlana may be too busy with business to bother much with editorial content. He owns cellular 'phone shares, is bidding for a R6bn state telecommunications contract jointly with two US telephone companies, and generally seems headed for a major niche in the

Continued on page 132

PETER SULLIVAN

Trick or treat

The most remarkable thing about editing a newspaper under the new dispensation is its normality, says the editor of *The Star*, the country's leading white-owned daily...

The challenges of editing a newspaper in the new South Africa are little different from those elsewhere: getting the latest news to readers, at the right time, at the right place and at the right price. But the normality of this is spectacularly unusual for those of us who were born — and learned journalism — under apartheid. Normality is abnormal — and delightful.

We were taught to criticise well for there was little good one could write or wanted to write about apartheid. In preferring criticism to praise we are not unlike other journalists around the world, but it was our single-mindedness which distinguished us, and it is here that we have to change.

We now have a government with which we interact normally, a government that gets angry with the press and our newspaper and also delights in what we say, a government that has as good an idea of press freedom as we have. We are learning to live with each other in the way normal democracies do and this can be painful.

For *The Star*, as the country's biggest and probably most influential daily paper, the problems of our new society become the problems of the newspaper: a crisis of expectation versus delivery, rising crime, transformation of business to better reflect the racial make-up of the country, corruption.

Perhaps President Mandela promised too much in the elections, but then that's what all politicians do and have done since the Greeks introduced democracy with its element of popularity linked to power. Now the many eager black people who hoped for quick, sharp change begin to grow restless — with their government, with their lack of material goods, with their newspaper.

We have to tell them it will not be happening soon and unfortunately we cannot give them the old solution we offered so readily of blaming the government. The new government is doing all right but not even the president's charm can give everyone houses, jobs, food and security. It will take time, but when the newspaper echoes the government on these questions readers ask whether we are now the Government of National Unity's lackeys.

It's tough, but then so are editors as a breed. ❏

GABU TUGWANA

Censorship by intimidation

... Not quite so, says the black editor of *New Nation*

Our independent weekly newspaper, *New Nation*, was born nine years ago, from the belly of a vicious censorship machine, which banned at least seven editions and shut down the publication for three months. Our founding editor, Zwelakhe Sisulu, was detained without trial for over two years; the state secret police repeatedly ransacked our offices; one of our photographers was unsuccessfully bribed to spy on us. All this in the name of preventing the newspaper from publishing material allegedly a threat to the maintenance of public order or likely to delay the termination of the State of Emergency under apartheid.

That is behind us now and we are promised human rights, a bill of rights and freedom of expression in the constitution now being mooted in the constitutional assembly.

But things are not yet plain sailing. Editing a newspaper during the process of change, you come face to face with the pains of change. In April, our reporter, Zohra Mohamed, wrote a story on the two convicted murderers of the late Umkhonto We Sizwe (the ANC military wing) chief of staff Chris Hani.

Mohamed's story revealed that Polish-born Janus Walusz who shot Hani and Clive Derby-Lewis, the Conservative Party (CP) member linked to the killing, were living comfortably on death row — still clinging to their right-wing views and showing no remorse for their actions a year later.

The Afrikaaner Weerstands-Beweging (AWB) issued a statement to a newspaper with strong right-wing sentiments saying that the *New Nation* article was 'anti-Boer bashing of the extreme kind and it (the AWB) has taken note of the journalist responsible for this evil story'. The AWB national executive claimed the story was 'by far the clearest example to date of the anti-white, inverted racist nature of some of the media in South Africa.'

The AWB's attempt to censor was repeated by Hinbo International, a Taiwanese clothing factory, with an attempt at financial intimidation by filing an urgent injunction with the Supreme Court to prevent *New Nation* from publishing an article on its inhuman working practices and the exploitation of local and illegal foreign immigrants. The court dismissed the case with costs to the applicants. Despite its lack of resources, Hinbo had reckoned without *The Nation*'s committment to free expression, forged in harder times than these. ❏

Continued from page 129

communications industry.

Other black business groups are after getting into the act. Black business magazine *Enterprise*, under former *Sowetan* staffer Thami Mazwai, is courting Swedish publishers about launching a national business newspaper for blacks. Real Africa Investments under Don Ncube, also listed on the JSE, is said to be in the market for TML.

There are changes, too, in ownership organisations. The Newspaper Press Union has merged with the Provincial Press Association and the Magazine Publishers Association to form the Print Media Association. The grouping, which previously functioned a bit like a sleepy old boys' club, is likely to change as Motlana and the new band of black owners continue to grow.

As the racial character of ownership becomes less of an issue, other matters are raising their heads: further foreign ownership, cross-ownership, and editorial independence.

The entry of Tony O'Reilly into the South African market is likely to be followed by others. There have been rumours of Conrad Black having an interest in TML. As satellite broadcasting becomes a reality for South Africa in mid-year, the Rupert Murdochs may come sniffing for print-broadcast synergies here. So far, there has been little discussion of the implications.

As the airwaves become re-regulated to allow for commercial and community radio and television, the Independent Broadcast Authority (IBA) is also conducting a major enquiry into cross-ownership, with the aim of developing a policy on this matter. The PMA opposes restrictions, although its provincial press component has asked for exemptions at its level in the event of restrictions. In the interests of investment and media growth, it is unlikely that the IBA will outlaw print-broadcast cross-ownership, though some conditions may be attached.

Meanwhile, the Argus company is involved with a company aiming to syndicate radio news to new stations, and the co-operatively-owned national press agency, SAPA, is doing likewise. It is uncertain whether cross-ownership regulations, if such materialise, will apply to such print-owned distributors (as opposed to broadcasters). Both TML and Argus are involved with online electronic information services.

In the meantime, M-Net/Multichoice — an encoded subscription-service TV network, run by former owners of the mainstream press — themselves have branched out into cellular telephony, and linked their existing newspaper shareholders with both Motlana and Ncube in the Mobile Telephone Networks (MTN) company. Through a tie-up with Swiss-based Richemont, M-Net/Multichoice has formed PayCo, with an estimated 1.35 million subscribers in Africa, Italy and the Benelux countries. The group is now poised to take advantage of impending satellite transmission to South Africa by distributing a range of international television services to holders of its decoders.

With the increasing competition, commercialisation and internationalisation in media ownership in South Africa, the question of editorial independence is coming to the fore. It was symbolised dramatically in print by Richard Steyn's resignation. Concerned journalists and editors are still looking at ways of keeping owners at bay; owners are moving to close down the Press Council, a body to whose standards editors could have referred in disputes with owners. The issue is likely to resurface. ❑

WEEKLY MAIL & GUARDIAN

JEFF ZERBST

Getting into bed with democracy

Pornography has replaced politics as the big issue in press freedom

A new era has dawned in South Africa. Social freedoms have accompanied political liberation, and the adult publishing industry has benefited enormously.

The dominant morality under National Party rule was sternly Calvinistic. To look at pictures of naked women was ungodly and depraved.

Indeed, it was also illegal. Pornographic magazines were banned in terms of the Publications Act of 1974, which outlawed such material on the grounds that it was obscene, and corrupted public morals.

In 1993, however, things started changing. Breasts which previously had to be covered with stars suddenly flopped pendulously into view. In August 1993, a new publication, *Hustler*, gave South Africa its first flash of pubic hair. That launch issue was immediately banned for being 'lewd, titillating, depraved, obscene, disgusting and sick'. These, and similar terms, continued to be used by the censors during the following 17 months.

From April 1994, however, the censors became progressively less sure of themselves as *Hustler* began challenging banning orders on the grounds that they were unconstitutional. (Other publications merely sat back and watched.)

South Africa, after all, now had an interim constitution in place which entrenched the decidedly unfamiliar principles of freedom of speech and expression. *Hustler* claimed that these principles applied directly to the publishing of soft-core pornography and argued that, even though the old Act was still on the statute books, it had now to be interpreted in the light of the new constitution.

This argument did not prove immediately decisive; the Directorate of Publications in Cape Town continued to ban every issue of *Hustler*. The Publications Appeal Board in Pretoria, however, was more open to persuasion. Over time, they accepted that freedom encompassed tolerance, and that tolerance no longer meant *that which the average South African could abide, but that which the average South African could tolerate other people looking at.*

Using this test as a yardstick, the Publications Appeal Board was — by the summer of 1994 — already in the habit of unbanning our issues on appeal. By this time *Hustler* was showing veritable bushes of pubic hair and even photographs in which vaginal lips were clearly visible. The chairman of the Appeal Board warned the publisher and editor that they were 'sailing as close to the wind as possible' but *Hustler*'s appeals kept succeeding.

Part of the reason for the board's more liberal attitude was that by August 1994, a Task Group appointed by Minister of Home Affairs, Chief Mangosuthu Buthelezi, had already started its work. Its brief was to draft new publications and film legislation which facilitated freedom of expression while at the same time protecting those citizens who did not wish to view such material.

> ' Every person shall have the right to freedom of speech and expression, which shall include freedom of the press and other media, and the freedom of artistic creativity and scientific research'
>
> *Interim Constitution*

Hustler, as an interested party, submitted a lengthy proposal to the Task Group. It recognised in its submission that certain limits on liberty should be accepted, and argued that child pornography, bestiality and sexual depictions incorporating violence should be outlawed. Outside those boundaries, it argued that no restriction should be placed on the depiction of full nudity in a consensual context.

The Task Group received hundreds of written submissions and listened to evidence from experts and ordinary members of the public in a number of major centres. Though conservative religious groups were particularly conspicuous by their presence at these hearings, their views did not win the day. An outline of proposed legislation published early in

1995 was extremely encouraging. While the Task Group acknowledged
the input of conservative elements, it accepted the argument that no clear
causal link has ever been established between pornography and violent
behaviour.

The proposed legislation was, in certain respects, more liberal than
even we had suggested. Child pornography was to be banned outright
but citizens could own S/M-type material, and material which depicted
bestiality. Distribution of such material, however, was still prohibited.

The Task Group accepted that the old publications legislation was
unconstitutional because it intruded on adults' freedom, gave preference
to the Judeo-Christian ethic and did not allow
enough latitude for artistic expression.

Sexually explicit

material is a welcome
It stipulated that adult publications would still
have to be sold in plastic wrappers with an
antidote to the
Adults Only warning on the cover. As before,
these magazines were only to be sold to people
repressive moral
of 18 and older.

climate that prevailed
From *Hustler*'s point of view this draft
legislation — which should be tabled during the
prior to the advent of
next parliamentary session — is acceptable apart
political and social
from one important stipulation. The proposed
law states that sexually explicit videos (those
freedom
which show intercourse) may not be distributed
through mail order. (This stipulation is no doubt
there to ensure that children who open their parents' post do not find
themselves in possession of an instant 'tool of corruption'.) *Hustler*
considers this a harsh injunction, and will, no doubt, challenge its
constitutionality in due course.

While the proposed legislation appears sensible for the most part, its
formulators sometimes say disturbing things. Professor Kobus van
Rooyen, an experienced censor who headed the Task Group, said in a
recent newspaper interview that publishers would not be permitted to
show erect penises!

This pronouncement is a throwback to old-style censorship and
reflects a ludicrously patriarchal orientation (showing a woman's private
parts is okay, but don't you dare show men in a state of barely controlled
arousal). If van Rooyen and his cohorts are going to insist on this
stipulation, *Hustler* will certainly be tangling with them shortly.

136   INDEX ON CENSORSHIP 3 1995

Hustler sees its future as being relatively secure as things stand today. Its future policy will be to show naked female and male forms in all their pristine beauty. It does not anticipate that the showing of penetration will be acceptable in the foreseeable future; it accepts that — for now — real sex will be confined to videos.

There is no doubt that the South African public loves *Hustler*. The latest circulation figures for magazines and newspapers in South Africa (July to December 1994) show that *Hustler* is the country's fastest growing publication (a rise of 61 per cent to an average sales figure of 152,000). *Penthouse* (90,000) and *Playboy* (83,000) were left trailing in its wake. Since that audit, *Hustler*'s sales have climbed to 175,000, and should hit the 250,000 mark within the next 12 months.

To be sure, one of the reasons *Hustler* has thrived in South Africa is that people have always been deprived of this type of material. But sexual titillation is only one part of the equation. *Hustler*'s black, irreverent humour has also drawn readers to it, as well as its willingness to make hard-hitting socio-political comments.

Many people were shocked, for example, when *Hustler* made Winnie Mandela its Asshole of the Month for August 1994. That seemed unacceptably irreverent to some, not to mention politically dubious. But Mrs Mandela's reputation has plummeted considerably since that article appeared, and South Africans are realising that true freedom of speech has few boundaries, and that all public figures are fair game for severe criticism and biting satire.

Hustler in South Africa has built up a rapid reputation for fearless straight talking. This championing of free speech, plus its highly visible role in facilitating legislative change in publishing, has enhanced its popularity and credibility.

Its defence of its right to publish is not restricted to legal argument, however. It believes that sexually explicit material is a welcome antidote to the repressive moral climate which prevailed prior to the advent of political and social freedom. The taboo on sexual information and depictions in South Africa is over. In answering the needs of its readers, *Hustler* is neither corrupting a nation nor creating sexual monsters.

On the contrary, it believes it is time for a formerly repressed nation to let go of its inhibitions and embrace freedom in its multifarious forms. Once in the seductive grip of democracy, South Africa's citizens will cling fervently to their accommodating new bedmate. ❏

CHRISTOPHER HOPE

Not the best of British

Many people are mad in South Africa. The long years of apartheid did it. The damage done to the principal victims is clear enough. Less well known is that it also sent many of those who ran the system around the bend. So numerous are they that you have to be pretty far gone to warrant attention in the New South Africa.

That's what drew me to the little town of Vosburg, in the heart of that vast, beautiful, remote, arid expanse of nothing very much but sheep and windmills, known as the Karoo, where some people are, quite literally, barking. They believe themselves to be the guardians of the Anglo-Saxon Heritage, descendants of Adam, the first man to blush, as well as relatives of the English royal family, and a lot more besides. Up and down the country there is much talk about the changes in South Africa since a democratically elected government came to power one year ago. It is city talk. The usual rhetoric sprayed at people in the hopes they will nod off. Seen from Vosburg, the changes in South Africa have been great, but not much has altered.

Later this year Vosburg celebrates its one-hundredth birthday. It is a pleasant little place, with a few hundred inhabitants, mostly Coloured, or Mixed Race people; and about 150 whites. It wins prizes for the prettiest policestation. Its single Victorian hotel, the Hunter's Home, is the best inn for many miles.

It should be happy, but happy it is not. And the reason is that the Israelites are coming to town. In Vosburg they have found the promised land. They seem modest people, and rather hardup, for an invading force. God will provide, the Israelites told me. But such modest finances may be deceptive. Someone who happens to have seen the bank statements of some of the group was astounded at the sums involved.

The Israelites are staging, coloured people in Vosburg maintain, an invasion; buying up cheap houses cheaply and spurning all contact. The

WEEKLY MAIL & GUARDIAN

white citizens of Vosburg are no less forthright. The local Afrikaans pastor of the Dutch Reformed Church is tearing his hair out; they're everywhere, they're trouble and they're poaching his flock.

In fact there are around 12 of them, a round apostolic dozen, and they've been moving into Vosburg and the nearby hamlet of Copperton, for the past few years. Mostly refugees from the big cities. Often they have left behind paying jobs in business, and guitars in hand, headed for the Karoo. The guitars are essential for Israelites compose most of their sacred music for services in each other's homes. Just like the early Christians, they told me, adding, rather confusingly, that they were not Christians.

The Israelites have names like Skinner and Robinson and Thompson and Eatwell — 'assumed names', as Mr Eatwell told me with a wry grin.

Well, I could understand that. If the Eatwells are descended from the wandering tribes of Israel, then Eatwell is not a likely name, is it? Something like Rabinowitz or Solomon would be closer to the truth, not so?

That was the first of many mistakes. The Israelites might not be Christians — but they are, well, British actually. But once upon a time they would have owned fully-fledged Israelite names, because the

a unique *opportunity* to write the *course* of **history.**

It's time for all South Africans to write the New Constitution. The following topics are presently under discussion at the Constitutional Assembly. The 490 elected members of the Constitutional Assembly would like to hear from you.

Theme Committee 5
(Judicial and Legal System)
1. Which courts should have constitutional jurisdiction?
2. Should there be any change to the structure of the Appeal Court, Constitutional Court, the Supreme Court and other courts?
3. How should judges be appointed?
4. What qualifications/attributes are required for appointment as a judicial officer?
5. To whom should the judiciary account?
6. How can access to courts by ordinary people be ensured?

Theme Committee 6
(Specialised structures of government)
SUB-THEME COMMITTEE 1
Should the functions of the public service be provided for in the new constitution? If yes, what details should be included?

SUB-THEME COMMITTEE 2
Constitutional provisions relating to the national revenue fund and procurement.

SUB-THEME COMMITTEE 3
PUBLIC PROTECTOR
Many countries have a Public Protector/Ombudsperson to investigate abuses and corruption by public officials in government.
Do we need a Public Protector/Ombudsperson in South Africa?
If yes, what should its role, function and powers be?

SUB-THEME COMMITTEE 4
POLICE: Provisions dealing with the police.

These are very important issues that will affect your life now – and for the future. To air your views, contact any member of the Constitutional Assembly, your organisation, or write direct to The Executive Director, Constitutional Assembly, P.O. Box 15, Cape Town 8000. Remember, the closing date for submissions is 10 March 1995. Do the write thing, and make your mark in the pages of history.

WEEKLY MAIL & GUARDIAN

Advertisement inviting the population to participate in writing the constitution

Skinners and Robinsons and the Eatwells of Vosburg believe themselves to be the descendants of the lost 10 tribes of Israel, which were dispersed across the world, to settle in Britain from where the 'heritage of the Anglo-Saxon' race had been wafted abroad to the benefit of native races around the globe. 'Mud people' Mr Eatwell calls them.

He has an Israelite family tree hanging on his wall. It begins with 12 tribes in Palestine, with Adam and Eve, and ends in Buckingham Palace with Queen Elizabeth on her throne, beneath which reposes — Mr Eatwell produces the surprise that lurks beneath the throne, with a conjurer's flourish — the sacred Stone of Scone! Sacred, that is, to the Israelites from the time of Abraham.

We are, Mr Eatwell confided, true sons of Adam — Adamites; quite literally — and he reaches for the Hebrew dictionary — a ruddy people, people of the red earth; people who can blush. Did I take his drift?

I did indeed. Mud people can't blush.

I went over to see Dave and Hillary, down the road. How did they feel about the other Israelites, those who lived in Israel? This was another gaffe. It turned out that the people living in Israel were not true Israelites at all. Impostors. Khazar Turks, said Dave.

Hillary lent me a book by their pastor, F W C Neser.

It was called *The Lost Ten Tribes of Israel*. In it I discovered that not only were the present-day Israelis charlatans; even more regrettably they were Jews — and Jews were responsible, together with the Free Masons, for a giant conspiracy to emasculate the western 'races' of the Anglo-Saxon world. Jews were also behind the New World Order, and the Babylonian confusion afflicting the Western world, especially South Africa. Jesus Christ had not been a Jew. This was a base lie. Jesus had been a tall blonde man of Anglo-Saxon appearance. And Jews, well, Jews had Jewish noses. Had anyone ever seen a picture of Jesus with a Jewish nose? There was a section on recognising Jewish noses, for the enquiring Israelite.

Some of this began to grow familiar. I had last visited Vosburg some three years earlier, and sitting in the bar of the Hunter's Home one Saturday afternoon, I had been told, by two white farmers, of a plot by the black races to sleep with whites in order 'to steal their genetic code'. I had been assured of the truths to be found in The Protocols of Zion, which exposed once and for all the conspiracy 'of international Jewry', the spawn of Satan. And I had been assured that the white citizens of Vosburg had no intention of accepting black children in their segregated school, or in the town, or in the bar of the Hunter's Home.

Three years later I began to understand a little better. At the time I imagined I was listening to an extreme version of the neo-fascist rant you can hear in any country bar on a hot afternoon. I had been wrong. The large, loud men who preached this peculiar sermon were the advance party of Israelites in Vosburg. And where they had led, others have followed.

And so far at least they appear to have chosen very well. The school remains white; and the Coloured people live outside town; and nothing, as far as I can see, has changed, in Vosburg. Except that the racist enthusiasm of some white inhabitants now has a religious basis. For the Israelites, who do not name the name of God, declare themselves to be the holy people of Yahweh — and once again the Hebrew dictionary comes out to persuade me that 'holy' means 'separate'. As well as 'sanctified in apartness'; a royal priesthood.

Now the curious thing about this is that it is not new, but old. It is, indeed, exactly the theological position, now spiked with large helpings of Hitlerian anti-Semitism, which the Afrikaner Dutch Reformed Church used to justify apartheid for as long as I can remember. The Israelites use the same scriptural underpinning to buttress their desire to stay separate from the 'hewers of wood and drawers of water', otherwise known as the mud-people.

The Afrikaans church has abandoned this position. But many of its followers have not. And the Israelites are the beneficiaries of deep divisions among the former ruling Afrikaner people. Little surprise then that the Dominee of Vosburg is at his wits' end. For the Israelites lure his congregation away by offering the same ethnic havens once provided by his own Church.

Vosburg says more about the new South Africa than any number of headlines and excited choruses of self-congratulatory clichés. In Vosburg, most people are brown, or coloured, and they have always had, still have, and will go on having, lots and lots of poverty. The white farmers of the district have lots and lots of land. In the year that has gone by since a new government came to power in South Africa, the only movement in Vosburg has been backwards.

I sometimes think that the white rulers of South Africa were not as slow as some would like to believe. Consider; for half a century it was considered normal to let the servants run the house and garden, on behalf of their white masters. Seen from the great country spaces, where most people in South Africa live, I wonder whether someone did not have a brainwave last April; and let them run the country on much the same basis. ❏

© Christopher Hope

CINEMA
FORBIDDEN

'Sight and Sound' offers the definitive chronicle of film and video censorship in Britain, from sexuality to drugs, politics to violence, blasphemy to criminal behaviour. Published free with the June issue, the 24-page full colour supplement charts the history of censorship, 1895-1995, from the banning of 'Battleship Potemkin' to the furore over the video release of Tarantino's 'Reservoir Dogs'.

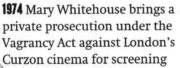
Sight and Sound

1913 The first Annual Report of the BBFC lists 'scenes tending to disparage public characters and institutions' and 'native customs in foreign lands abhorrent to British ideas' as reasons for banning films
1943 Churchill fails to have production of 'The Life and Death of Colonel Blimp' halted on the grounds of its alleged mockery of the military officer protagonist. The BBFC passes the film, but it is cut for export to allied nations
1974 Mary Whitehouse brings a private prosecution under the Vagrancy Act against London's Curzon cinema for screening

'Blow Out'. The case is dismissed
1987 The first two 'Rambo' films are blamed for the Michael Ryan killings in Hungerford. The BBFC cuts over one minute from the theatrical version of 'Rambo III'
1993 D.W. Griffith's 'The Birth of a Nation' (1915) is passed '15' on video and a caption is added by the BBFC to contextualise the film's presentation of the Ku Klux Klan

June issue on sale now

DIARY

YELENA BONNER

Sorry? Are you Jewish?

Self-determination is a very private matter, a question of personal identity. To write about it is to write about oneself

In 1936, or early 1937 perhaps, there was a population census. The papers said that you could answer the question about nationality just as you pleased. I can't remember the exact phrasing, but that was how we all understood it. This was when I discovered that the problem (and the category) of nationality even existed. But in the Comintern building where I was brought up, the division of children and teenagers into friendly and inimical factions, was rooted in other factors. This was true of adults too. The one thing that everyone really knew about anyone else was whether they were Soviet or foreign — from the United States, Poland, Bulgaria, Portugal, or Austria. And then there were those of us who came from a mixed background: a Soviet mother, a Chinese father. But that year many of us were planning to be Spanish. And my best friend Seva Bagritsky said that he was German-Jewish. I was a bit put out by this, but then it seemed funny. All this passion for national identity couldn't have been serious though, because I can't remember what I called myself at the time.

In 1938 I had my age assessed by a medical commission because I had no birth certificate. I was expected to fill in a questionnaire which indicated the nationality of my parents. I wrote that my mother was Jewish and my father Armenian (there was no need for strangers to know that he was my stepfather, after all). The fact that my real father, whom I

KARSH OF OTTAWA/CAMERA PRESS

Yelena Bonner and husband Andrei Sakharov, who died in 1989

had seen three times (and was to see once more during the war), was also Armenian was considered coincidental. Along with my passport I now had a nationality: I was 'Armenian'. Later on it surprised me that I hadn't been aware of anti-Semitism until I joined the army, and that this was the first time I was touched by its darker side.

In the winter of 1941, a few days before the new year, I was sitting on a bench in the darkened corridor of the Sverdlovsk evacuation centre waiting to hear where they would send me. I had been wounded, hospitalised and ordered back into action. I felt no urge at all to 'fight for my country'. There was a stark coldness in my stomach, fear of the future and the insistent memory of freezing hands and feet, the sensation of congealed menstrual bandages unchanged for days rubbing against my thighs. A man sat down beside me, a soldier. They were all soldiers there. 'Ex nostris?' he asked. I failed to understand. 'Sorry?' 'One of us?' 'One of who?' 'Are you Jewish?' I answered: 'Yes — well, no. My mother's Jewish. I'm a Muscovite from Leningrad.' He said 'Let's hear about it.' 'What?' 'Everything.' So I told him. That I was just out of hospital. That I lived in Moscow. That my mother and father had been arrested. My brother and I had come to Leningrad to stay with our grandmother. My uncle had been arrested. There were now three of us at our grandmother's because uncle's wife had been deported to Katta-Kurgan. I didn't like Leningrad. Before the war it had been a place of exile to me, like Katta-Kurgan or mama's Alzhir. But now I wanted to go to Leningrad more than anything else because that was where my grandmother was dying with the two children. And I'd been here since the morning. And I was very thirsty, because they had given me dry rations of bread and herring and I had devoured the lot. And the water in my flask wasn't just metallic, it stank. I concluded my monologue as suddenly as I had begun, anxious that I didn't know why I was saying all this and to whom. He said: 'Where is Alzhir?' and I explained that it was the Akmolinsky camp for the wives of traitors to the country. He said, 'I want to go to Leningrad too. More than anything else. I have a wife there, a son and daughter. How old are you?' 'I'll be 19 in February.' 'She'll be 18.' He rose and said, 'Stay here. Don't go away.' And he set off down the corridor. After a few steps he turned back. He removed a piece of paper and a pencil from his map-case and held them out to me. 'Write down your name and year of birth.' I rested the sheet of paper on a copy of *Evgeny Onegin* which I had taken out of my bag that morning. I hadn't opened it once. I wrote my name and handed back the sheet. He read it out loud: 'Bonnyer, Yelena Georgievna'. And as though to confirm it he said: 'Reading *Onegin* are you?' 'It's Bonner,' I said. 'Actually I'm learning it by heart.' 'The whole thing?' 'Yes.' 'What else will you be learning then?' 'Akhmatova. From the six-volume edition.' 'Test you this evening.' He spent a good hour or more wandering the labyrinthine corridors of the evacuation centre, disappeared somewhere into its depths, returned to the room next door and finally emerged with some papers. He put them into the map-case and, slipping his hands into the sleeves of the overcoat he carried with him, said, 'All right, let's go, nurse Yelena Georgievna Bonner of medical train number 122.' We stepped out into the icy, creaking street. I asked him why he insisted on carrying his overcoat wherever he went. Was he afraid that I'd steal it? There was no black-out

In 1945...I became a Jew. What else could I call myself when, after war with the Germans, a war against 'murderous Jewish doctors' was declared

in Sverdlovsk, but there was no lighting either and December days are short. I saw him blush in the dark. He began making excuses saying that he hadn't understood, that I mustn't take offence and that I should trust him. He said that he had trusted me right away and had taken me on as a nurse even though he understood perfectly well that with my ROKK (Russian Red Cross) courses I was nothing of the sort. I said that I already trusted him anyway and had asked out of caprice. But he continued, 'Can you write out first-aid prescriptions for 60 wounded?' 'I don't know.' 'Can you find a vein?' 'I've never done intravenous injections.' 'So what have you done?' 'Bandages. Splints. Tourniquets. Morphine. Carried the dead.' 'Fine. You'll have to learn the rest in a fortnight.' 'Why a fortnight?' 'That's how long we're likely to be hanging around before the wounded are brought in.' We got into a tram. At the station we got out. We walked for a long time along the empty tracks. The fear that wouldn't leave me in the corridors of the evacuation centre was transformed into a hope that I would drink hot tea and sleep on the bunk of a railway carriage listening to the rattle of wheels, as I had slept when they transported me, heavily wounded (the slightly wounded were not granted this privilege) from the Vologodsk evacuation hospital to Sverdlovsk. And I asked him, 'Did you take me on as a nurse because I'm Jewish?' He answered, 'And why not?' I said nothing. And when, in silence, we had reached the train, he said, 'Here we are. This is home. My name's Vladimir Efremovich but you'll be calling me comrade commander. I took you because you're Jewish. And so that you'd survive.' So I became a nurse.

I was helped by the senior operations nurse, Taisia Ivanovna, whom I didn't like much but admired immensely for her professionalism, and by the chief pharmacist Anna Andreevna, the dearly loved eldest member of the team. After that I became a senior nurse in medical train number 122, then the head of the medical section of the engineering battalion. I survived. And I remained myself. Thanks to him.

I decided to call myself a Jew during a wild outbust of Armenian anti-Semitism with all those trivial officers' anecdotes and stories about Jews fighting in Tashkent. It was after one great military commander coined the phrase 'the lovely Sarah' which stuck among the junior nurses: it was supposed to refer to me. And after Vladimir Efremovich received news of the death of his son Efim, a little boy who had barely finished his ninth

DMITRY PEISAKHOV/CAMERA PRESS

Soviet Jews remember, 1991: commemoration of the 1941 massacre of Jews at Babi Yar

year at school. I am still devastated by the fact that I couldn't persuade Vladimir Efremovich to take him on our train, and convince him that he was wrong to say that he couldn't do it because this was his son and because he was Jewish.

I considered myself a Soviet officer long after demobilisation with some degree of pride, or vanity perhaps. But I never identified with Russian national feeling, even though I knew no other language and culture. I still didn't consider myself Russian. Though others sometimes did.

One golden autumn day in 1967, I was walking down Marszalkowska Street in Warsaw and asked a passer-by for directions to the Hotel Bristol. A Polish friend saw this from a distance. When we met up he remarked, 'I fear that, with a naivety characteristic of Russian occupiers, you assume that everyone here should understand you.' Did this reflect a tension associated with the massive emigration — or expulsion, rather — of the Jews from Poland at the time? Was it an expression of the age-old wound inflicted upon the Poles by Russia? But I felt a sense of guilt. Was I an occupying officer? Was I Russian?

It was the end of August 1968. I was staying with my mother's sister in Paris. I felt totally indifferent to Paris, the boulevards, the museums, even Nika Samofrakiiskaya. I was tormented by pain, shame and guilt. I thought the whole country was suffering as I was; that I must return to Moscow, and my return ticket was only for 15 September. Every day I had to meet new members of the family. The wife of a second cousin came to visit with a 12-year-old boy. He stepped into the room and stood silently by the wall. 'Why won't you say hello to your cousin?' they asked. He looked me steadily in the eye and said: 'I don't shake hands with a Russian officer.' I don't know what they had told him about my rank. But even without him I knew that the tanks in Prague were my tanks. And I felt ashamed. I was guilty.

In August 1945, I received a new military card (that damn 'nationality' category again) and I became a Jew. The discrepancy with my passport didn't matter. What else could I call myself when, after war with the Germans, a war against 'cosmopolitans' and 'murderous Jewish doctors' was declared. I allowed myself to weaken just once. My 'Notes of a Doctor' were published in the journal *Neva* in 1962. I signed them with the double-barrelled name Bonner-Alikhanova (the second name was my stepfather's; I had used it as a child). My closest friend was furious and said that I was covering up my Jewishness with it. If it had been anyone else the whole thing would have faded without trace. Instead 'our' press represented me as an agent of international Zionism. There were endless telephone calls: 'Just wait you bloody Jew.' In recent years this has alternated with the question: 'You still alive then, you old Armenian hag?' I've no idea what I would have heard if those who rang had known that the Kurds regard me as half-Kurdish, and that the Lithuanians had given me a Lithuanian independence medal.

There was a particularly interesting conversation on 19 August 1993. A woman telephoned and asked for Yelena Georgievna, saying pleasantly who she was and that she was a Muscovite. I said I was delighted and that I was a Muscovite too. Her answer was littered with the unprintable: 'A Muscovite? You? Jewish bitch. Get out of our city.' I didn't hear where I was supposed to go. I put down the receiver. And I remembered what other Muscovites had been...

In the winter of 1943, our train was sent off to Irkutsk for repair; it was half burnt out, full of holes, with no window panes after the bombing. We were temporarily based at the hospital. I was walking back after my shift, towards the bridge which crossed the river Angara. In the dim light falling from the windows of the single-storey houses on the outskirts of the city — the sparse snowflakes flashed brightly. And somewhere ahead a clear childish voice chanted: 'I have spoken wherever I go,/ Of my city, of Moscow the golden.' On the bench sat a girl of about eight, wrapped in a white scarf and a little boy of about six. When I came up she fell silent. I asked her what she had been singing. She answered that it was a new song. It had been sung on the radio three times and she had managed to remember it. It was about Moscow. 'I am a Muscovite,' she added. Then she asked, 'And you?' 'I am too,' I said. 'Sing it again.' And she did. Once, twice, three times. I remembered it after three hearings as well. 'I've been roving the world all alone,/ Know what sadness and yearning can bring.' I found the word 'roving' grated a bit because it seemed too light and incongruous in our context. But that was secondary. The main thing was that I suddenly rediscovered what I had nearly lost. It was quite clear: I was a Muscovite.

On 23 August 1991 my friends and those of my children, company 401 of the living ring that had defended the White House, were celebrating our victory. We ate. We drank. We sang the ballads of Galich, Okudzhava, Vysotsky. And suddenly, we heard a long-forgotten song unfamiliar to this generation, you would have thought, which took us back to the years of the war. 'I have learned to be proud and beholden,/ I have spoken wherever I go,/ Of my city, of Moscow the golden/ That I'll cherish my whole life through.' Moscow... Muscovites...

Life is a series of episodes. Our memory selects them and spins Ariadne's thread — one for each of us. We all have our own labyrinth and must find our own way. My own thread has been drawn out over 70 years.

I am a Muscovite.

© Yelena Bonner *Translated by Irena Maryniak*

BABEL

Continuing our series focusing on the voices of those silenced by poverty, prejudice and exclusion

KIM TŎKCHIN

I have much to say to the Korean government

The story of the Asian women — up to 200,000 and dominantly Korean — abducted, coerced or seduced from home with promises of employment to serve as 'comfort women' for Japanese front-line troops, is one of the best-kept secrets of World War II. The Japanese destroyed the evidence, the USA condoned the cover-up while using Japan as the cornerstone of its regional Cold War balance, the Korean authorities remained silent in the interests of postwar harmony. For 50 years, the women, too, remained silent. Even on their return home they were shunned and ostracised in a patriarchal society where the 'shame' of a woman brought shame to the family and nation. Only in 1991, following the discovery of military documents in Japan, did the first of the victims, Kim Haksun, break the silence. The Korean Council for Women Drafted for Military Sexual Slavery by Japan was founded in the same year and encouraged other women to come forward. Their stories were harrowing, confirming in intimate detail the evidence of the documents above. The testimony of Kim Tŏkchin is one of 19 accounts collected by the Korean Council and published in 1993 in Korean as *Kangjero kkŭllyŏgan Chosnin kunwianbudul* (Comfort Women: Korean survivors of Japanese forced prostitution tell their stories). *JVH*

INDEX ON CENSORSHIP 3 1995   151

I was born in South Kyŏngsang Province, in 1921. My family owned no land that they could till, and they found it extremely difficult to live. So we went to my uncle's home. He made a living making bamboo baskets at the foot of Chiri Mountain. There, my father began to cultivate tobacco. Tobacco was a government monopoly. The leaves my father grew were sold to the government, and my father received only a small amount of money. After the main crop was harvested, new shoots sprang up from the tobacco stalks and he would dry these small leaves and smoke them himself. He continued to put the dried leaves aside until he was caught by the Japanese police. He was taken to the police station and subjected to a heavy beating. As a result of this, he took to his bed and eventually died. Mother had to carry on life with the five of us — two elder brothers, one elder sister, one younger sister and myself. We were desperate for food. We dug up the roots of trees to eat, and my mother would work on a treadmill all day to bring back a few husks of grains as payment which we would boil with dried vegetables for our supper. Those who flattered the Japanese were able to get help from them. But those who kept firmly apart were forced into extreme poverty...

It was the beginning of February, 1937. I was 17 years old. I heard a Korean man was in the area recruiting girls to work in the Japanese factories. I went to P'yŏngch'on to meet him and promised him I would go to Japan to work. He gave me the time and place of my departure. All I knew — all I thought I knew — was that I was going to work in a factory to earn money. I went to the bus stop in Ŭiryŏng as I had been instructed to do. The man who had come to recruit us took 30 of us to Pusan. Some were older, some were younger than me, and some were married with children. The married women told me that their husbands were already in Japan. We were all to stay together until our return to Korea...

We transferred to a public slow train and travelled slowly down to Pusan, where we boarded a boat. The boat was a ferry and took many other passengers. The crew brought us bread and water, and we sailed to Nagasaki. At Nagasaki, a vehicle resembling a bus came and took us to a guest-house. From that moment on we were watched by soldiers. I asked one of them: 'Why are you keeping us here? What kind of work are we going to do?' He simply replied that he only followed orders. On the first night there I was dragged before a high-ranking soldier and raped. He

KOREAN COUNCIL FOR WOMEN DRAFTED FOR MILITARY SEXUAL SLAVERY BY JAPAN

Crossing the Yellow River, 1940s: the snap that started the search in 1962, when Senda Kako, a Japanese journalist with Mainichi Shimbun, *discovered this photograph in the Japanese War Archives. On discovering there were comfort women from Korea, he began the first research into forced prostitution during World War II*

had a pistol. I was frightened at seeing myself bleed and tried to run away. He patted my back and said that I would have to go through this experience whether I liked it or not, but that after a few times I would not feel so much pain. We were taken here and there to the rooms of different high-ranking officers on a nightly basis. Every night we were raped. On the fifth day, I asked one of the soldiers: 'What is our work? Is it just going to bed with different men?' He replied: 'You will go wherever orders take you. And you will know what your job is when you get there.' We left Nagasaki after a week of this gruelling ordeal.

Led by Korean guides, we boarded another boat for Shanghai... We travelled for a few days then disembarked at what we were told was Shanghai.

There was a truck waiting for us at the pier. We passed through disordered streets and arrived in a suburban area. There was a large house right beside an army unit. The house was pretty much derelict and inside was divided into many small rooms. There were two Japanese women and about 20 Koreans there, so with the 30 of us who had arrived from Ŭiryŏng there were about 50 women in total. These two Japanese were said to have come from brothels. The soldiers preferred us Korean girls, saying we were cleaner. From the 50 of us, excluding those who were ill or had other reasons, 35 girls on average worked each day.

When the troops moved to the next place, what would happen would be that the comfort station, along with us women, would follow shortly afterwards. The comfort station was always positioned in a remote place, and our living conditions were practically the same wherever we went. We heard guns firing every day. There were bodies lying all over the place, and dogs would drag corpses around. We wore skirts and blouses of the sort that are quite common today, but we were given heavier clothes for winter.

We rose at seven in the morning, washed, and took breakfast in turns. Then from about nine o'clock the soldiers began to arrive and form orderly lines. From six o'clock in the evening high-ranking officers came, some of whom stayed over night. Each of us had to serve an average of 30 to 40 men each day, and we often had no time to sleep. When there was a battle, the number of soldiers who came declined. In each room there was a box of condoms which the soldiers used. There were some who refused to use them, but more than half put them on without complaining. I told those who would not use them that I had a terrible disease, and it would be wise for them to use a condom if they didn't want to catch it. Quite a few would rush straight to penetration without condoms, saying they couldn't care less if they caught any diseases since they were likely to die on the battlefield at any moment. On such occasions I was terrified that I might actually catch venereal disease. After one use, we threw the condoms away; plenty were provided.

About once every two months, an army surgeon gave us checkups. If any of us had a problem, she was ordered to rest for a few days. We had to go to the army hospital for checkups. At the hospital, there was an examination table on which we were made to lie with our legs spread wide apart. If we had any disease we would be given the 'No. 606' injection, but I was never diagnosed as needing such an injection. Yet, even though I had no venereal disease, I had to have treatment, because I kept bleeding and couldn't pass water. Perhaps it was a bladder infection. There were some women whose vaginas were so swollen and were bleeding so profusely that there was no space for a needle to be inserted inside. How could one expect anything to be otherwise when an innocent girl was subjected to such torture day and night? None of us had children, but I heard that some became pregnant and were forced to abort with an injection or with drugs. I have been told at a recent checkup that my womb is malformed due to the abusive use it received in my youth.

When I was in pain and distress I tried to die, but I couldn't. I thought of jumping into the river, jumping down from a high place or running into a car, but I never managed to do anything remotely like this. Whenever I was in such a sombre mood, I missed my mother greatly. And, even though I wanted to run away, it wasn't possible since I didn't know the area where I was being held. So I gave up any hope and I didn't rebel. I was so scared that I did whatever I was told to. Maybe because of this, the soldiers didn't treat me as cruelly as they could have done.

The gifts of my days as a comfort woman still trouble me. I have bladder infections, womb diseases, a restlessness of mind and many other ailments

There were some who fought against the men. Some were beaten and kicked by the soldiers. But I don't remember being hit, slapped or cursed.

Soldiers who returned from the battlefield were wild. They would try not to use condoms. The soldiers who were about to leave for combat were somewhat more gentle and a few of them would give us their loose change, saying it wouldn't be of any use to them if they died. There were even some who wept, they were so scared to go to fight. I would comfort them. When any returned alive, I could be genuinely glad to see them again. I acquired quite a few regular customers, and one or two confessed their love to me and even proposed...

Pretty and intelligent girls were selected for very high-ranking officers and taken into the army unit by car. I was chosen in this way and developed a special relationship with an officer called Izumi. When I asked how old he was, he spread five fingers before me, and so I guess he must have been about 50 years old. He seemed to be of quite a high standing. Izumi's room was large, and in it was a large bed, a shining gun and his neat uniform. When there was no combat taking place and things were calm, he used to send for me and keep me in his room for two or three days. When there was combat going on, I didn't hear from him for several months at a time, until the situation quietened down. Then he would call for me frequently once more. When his troops were moved away and his base was a distance to the comfort station, he took me with him by boat. One day as I was crossing a river to meet him, I saw the river dyed red with blood and bristling, crowded with bodies from bank to bank that parted on either side of us as our boat crept forward.

I came to regard Izumi almost as my father, husband and family rolled into one. Guiding my hand in his, he taught me numbers and how to write Japanese script, and through it all I could feel great affection. Everyday, he said he loved me. He said that when the war was over he would take me to Japan where I could live an easy life. He said that I would go to school and live with him. Even after I returned to Korea, we wrote to each other for quite some time

About three years after I had become a comfort woman, in February or March 1940, Izumi said that I should go back home since my health was getting worse just as the war was becoming more serious. He promised that he would come for me when the war was over. He asked if I had any friends with whom I would like to go home to Korea. I named four. Izumi ordered the manager to let me and these four return home. Izumi sent someone to escort us, and the five of us left the comfort station. Izumi offered to settle payment for our services later. He instructed us never to return. We didn't receive any money from the comfort station, but Izumi gave me 100 yen as we left.

After about 20 days of travelling, I got home. I was 20 by this time.

In my home, people seemed to be talking about me behind my back and we were still very poor, so I left and came up to Seoul. I lived by working in a guest-house or as a housemaid. For a time I worked in a factory making bags, then I ran a small shop. Just before the Korean war, I met a man whose wife had been left behind in Sariwŏn, in part of what had become North Korea. He was living alone with his children, and soon I moved in with him. Then during the war, his wife managed to escape southwards and started to live with her parents-in-law. Her husband continued to live away from her with his children and me. We sent his children through school. His son went to university and still writes to me, although he now lives in Los Angeles in America. The wife lives with her daughter now. She and I got on well right from the start and we are still on good terms. I had two sons and a daughter with this man, but my daughter died during the Korean War, and I am now living with my eldest son...

The gifts of my days as a comfort woman still trouble me. I have bladder infections, womb diseases, a restlessness of mind and many other ailments. I suffer from a gallstone and also have severe anaemia. Since I registered with the Council [For Women Drafted for Military Sexual Slavery by Japan] I have been feeling oppressed whenever I am indoors. The four of us, my son and his children, live in one crowded rented room in a terraced house in Puch'ŏn.

Until now I have lived with all my resentment and anger buried deep in my heart. But the television programmes about the Council left me unable to sleep at night. I went to one of my nephews, a high school teacher, whom I had helped to educate. I told him about my past and asked if I should register at the Council... He pleaded with me not to register. I discussed the matter with another nephew living in Taejŏn. He wept as he listened to my story and advised me not to register. He said, 'It will break your son's heart. What will your stepson in the United States say when he hears all this?' But I felt uneasy and couldn't sleep at all. So one day I went to a broadcasting station and told my story. I came home and slept soundly. I told my son about the whole thing, and he wept uncontrollably, saying, 'Mother, you have lived so courageously even with such a rough past. I am proud of you.' My heart moves more and more towards the meetings of the Council.

Of course Japan is to blame, but I resent the Koreans who were their instruments even more than the Japanese they worked for. I have so much to say to my own government. The Korean government should grant us compensation... ❏

© Kim Tŏkchin
© Korean Council for Women Drafted for Military Sexual Slavery by Japan

Excerpted from True Stories of the Korean Comfort Women *edited by Keith Howard (Cassell, August 1995)*

LEGAL: WAR CRIMES TRIBUNALS

**A legal column dedicated to the memory of Bernie Simons
(1941-1993), radical lawyer and defender of human rights**

CAROLINE MOOREHEAD

Truth with justice

Sometime late in June 1992, a group of young Bosnian Serbs, acting as camp guards at a concentration camp set up for Muslims in the mining complex of Omarska, called for a number of men prisoners to come to them in the mine's old garage. These Muslim prisoners had already been starved, beaten and humiliated, and several had watched their wives and sisters raped; but at least, unlike many of Omarska's other inmates, they were still alive. One of the guards was a man called Dusan Tadic, from Kozarac, near Prijedor, where many thousands of Muslims had been driven from their homes in the previous month. Tadic, also known as Dule or Dusko, began by beating three of the prisoners with metal rods, truncheons and knives; he stopped only when all three were unconscious. He then beckoned to a fourth prisoner, a man the records identify only as 'G'. G was ordered to grunt like a pig and then drink a can of motor oil. Then Tadic told him to bite off the testicles of the unconscious men, one of whom

revived sufficiently to scream with pain. All of them, by the time Tadic and his friends had finished with them, were dead.

That the details of such a horrendous story can be related, is a measure of the extent to which, in the 1990s, the world has become inured to routine atrocities. Only savagery of this nature still has the power to shock. As it is, Tadic, a 39-year-old former karate instructor, now stands accused as an 'accomplice to genocide', on 10 counts of murder and 15 of genocide, under international humanitarian laws variously embedded in or borrowed from the 1949 Geneva Conventions, the Hague Conventions of 1907 on the laws and customs of war, the Genocide Convention of 1948 and the Charter of the Military Tribunal of 1945.

What makes Dusan Tadic's story different from those of countless other tales of mutilation, sadism and murder perpetrated by all sides in the four-year conflict in former Yugoslavia is not, however, its savagery. Brutality of this kind has become commonplace in our time. Tadic is remarkable because he is the first person to be brought to trial before the new International Criminal Tribunal for the former Yugoslavia. Over two years of intensive work and preparation have at last yielded a single case. Recognised in Munich by a Muslim former inmate of Omarska camp in February 1994, Tadic was arrested by the German police and has been extradited to stand trial in the Hague, where the Tribunal has made its home in an old insurance building. Its prosecutor is Richard Goldstone, the South African judge known for his investigation into the deaths and injuries caused by the South African police when they fired into a crowd of 50,000 demonstrators; there are 11 judges, two trial chambers and one appeals chamber, and a staff of 160. Twenty-four cells, in a nearby prison, have been set aside for those summoned to appear. To comply with the demands of the new Tribunal, Germany changed its extradition laws to allow foreigners, though not nationals, to be taken outside the country to stand trial. (Denmark has chosen to try war criminals from the former Yugoslavia in its own courts, sending a 31-year-old Bosnian Muslim, Refic Saric, to prison for eight years after finding him guilty of torturing people to death in a Croatian prisoner-of-war

There have never, before today, been international trials for genocide and this fact alone makes them crucial

camp. Saric is currently in a psychiatric unit.)

Tadic may, as it turns out, also be the only war criminal to appear before the Tribunal. Of the 22 people so far indicted on the basis of overwhelming evidence of atrocities, all the others are believed to be in hiding somewhere in former Yugoslavia. The hundreds, even thousands, of others guilty of similar crimes, in a conflict in which civilians were made into deliberate targets with the specific aim of creating ethnically 'pure' territories, are no more likely to be found; while the Bosnian Serb leaders, Radovan Karadzic, Ratko Mladic and Mico Stanisic, who have now been named by the UN Tribunal as war crime suspects, have made it clear that they do not recognise the Tribunal's authority.

After stories emerged in the summer of 1992 about 11 Serbian-controlled prison camps in the occupied territories of Bosnia, where civilian men, women and children were being tortured and killed in the name of 'ethnic cleansing', the UN Security Council adopted Resolution 771. This expressed their 'grave alarm' about what was happening, and called on states and international organisations to collect more evidence. A warning was issued to the killers. On 6 October 1992, the Security Council set up a five member Commission of Experts, under

BENOIT GYSEMBERGH/CAMERA PRESS

Inside the Bosnian camps 1992: victims of Serbian war criminals

Chicago lawyer Cherif Bassiouni. After its report, with its clear findings of mass expulsions, killings, rape, torture, arbitrary arrests and pillage, the Security Council set up, in February 1993, the International Criminal Tribunal, not only to punish all those responsible for the atrocities, but to 'help restore and maintain the peace'. In order to avoid the dangers of having its work sabotaged, the Tribunal was set up, not as a treaty, which would have called for ratifications it had no possibility of getting, but as an enforcement measure, which, under Chapter VII, binds all states to comply with whatever the Security Council demands of them. The Tribunal has been given a temporal dimension — crimes committed only after 1 January 1991 — and a geo-graphical one — the territory covered by former Yugoslavia. Its brief is to supplement, not replace, the work of existing national courts.

The history of war crimes tribunals goes back to the fourteenth century, when a murderous French baron massacred the entire population of a village under siege, then pleaded that he had only been obeying the orders of his superior, one of the Dukes of Burgundy. Right up until 1944, under British law at least, obedience to superior orders proved sufficient to escape individual responsibility for war crimes. It was only at Nuremberg and Tokyo that individual culpability — with mitigation when it came to sentencing — was upheld. At the Hague, individuals are held responsible for every criminal act they have committed.

In the mid-1960s, the 93-year-old Bertrand Russell sought to make the USA accountable for its 'brutal treatment' of the people of Vietnam over 12 years by setting up a War Crimes Tribunal to try President Johnson and Dan Rusk. A jury of distinguished people, among them the French philosopher Jean-Paul Sartre, the Yugoslav partisan Vladimir Dedyer and Isaac Deutscher, met first at Stockholm, then at Roskilde in Denmark, to hear evidence of napalm bombing and the massacre of civilians from witnesses brought over from Vietnam. The proceedings were widely discredited in the press — Bernard Levin called Russell a decrepit puppet, immeasurably old and immeasurably frail, gullible and filled with rancorous hatred of all things American — and further disrupted by the antics of Russell's young Mephistopheles, Ralph Schoenmann. Though the stories brought from Vietnam were amply corroborated long before the disclosures about My Lai, the Tribunal closed under a cloud of public scepticism, and Russell's dreams of seeing it translated into a permanent court, where international injustices could be tried, if not before the law then at least before the world, evaporated after a number of lacklustre hearings in Rome.

Russell was not, of course, the only man to have such a dream. The last 40 years have seen repeated attempts by the UN International Law Commission to prepare drafts statutes for a permanent tribunal.

None have taken shape. One question now being asked is how far the Yugoslav experience will influence the nature of things to come, and whether it might carry in its wake a more lasting body.

Its most important repercussion to date is to be found in Rwanda, where, on 8 November 1994, the UN Security Council set up a second International Tribunal, to try people for what is now universally accepted to have been the planned genocide of the entire Tutsi population, involving acts of exceptional barbarity, like the beheading and mutilating of small children, extreme even by hardened contemporary standards. Judge Goldstone is again Prosecutor. The Rwanda Tribunal is to sit at Arusha, in neighbouring Tanzania.

In January, the first six investigators arrived in Kigali and began their enquiries. Given that witnesses are widely scattered, that many have been intimidated, that little documentary evidence exists, that graves have to be exhumed and examined by teams of forensic experts, and that proof has grown cold with the long delays, their task is awesome. Some say too awesome, that they have left it too long. Another major difficulty in Rwanda remains the very credibility of the UN itself, which pulled its peacekeepers out just as the genocide was beginning, and whose presence ever since has been marked by dilatoriness, inefficiency and a lack of funds or real commitment.

Rwanda's own efforts at bringing the guilty to trial have been hampered by an almost total lack of manpower, money and expertise. Having announced, shortly after taking power in mid-July, that they intended to prosecute all those accused of killings, the new government was obliged to recognise that, with only 200 magistrates, 12 prosecutors, and 36 criminal investigators to have survived the massacres, it was in no position to carry through its plans. Nor has the international community proved helpful, preferring generally to dwell on the undisputed hardship of the 29,000 Hutu detainees held indefinitely in overcrowded open-air compounds, than to honour pledges to provide help made while the Rwandan tragedy was on the front pages.

Without this injection of help, both legal and financial, it is highly improbable that the Rwandan government will be able to follow in the footsteps of Ethiopia, where a Special Prosecutor's Office has been set up to bring to trial the perpetrators of the abuses practised under President Mengistu. Gathering evidence against the 1,500 or so suspects currently in detention has been made considerably easier by the fact that Mengistu, like the Nazis in World War II, favoured the keeping of meticulous records, and that these incriminating documents fell into the hands of the opposition forces as they took power. The standards being set and observed by the Special Prosecutor's Office are reported to be extremely high.

What makes the judicial blockage in Rwanda the more frustrating is that even if Goldstone and his Tribunal do manage to assemble suffi-cient evidence to start hearing cases before too long, they have already announced that they are unlikely to be able to process more than 20 people each year. Though they will belong to the 400 or so 'key killers' of Rwanda's genocide, these men, like their Yugoslav counterparts, are beyond the reaches of the law, living over the border in Kenya, Zaire and Tanzania.

As with Yugoslavia, the difficulty is catching men in countries from which they may be extradited. Alfred Musema, the director of a tea factory in Gisovu, is accused of being a key player in the planning of the genocide, which left all but 400 or so of the 5,000 Tutsi population round his tea factory massacred by the Hutu militia. Musema, in hiding in Switzerland, was recognised and has been arrested. In May, two other suspected killers were arrested in Belgium, Vincent Ntezimana and Alphonse Higaniro. Rakia Omaar of African Rights, author of a remarkable report on the Rwandan genocide, questioned witnesses in Rwanda about these two men not long ago. Ntezimana, a former lecturer at the National University of Rwanda at Butare, was, she said, known to have collaborated with the Hutu killers and to have led them to the homes of colleagues on death lists. Meanwhile Higaniro, the former director of a match factory, surrounded himself with extremists who talked of putting Tutsis and moderate Hutu 'into a boiler' and turning his factory into a centre for the killers.

A Serbian camp guard and three

Rwandans, are to stand trial for so many thousands of murderers and torturers; four men, for how much tragedy? In Rwanda, 14 per cent of the entire population are dead, and countless others mutilated, raped and

Milosevic or Karadzic, are dim. The comparison with Nuremberg is important: though the Tribunal itself was different, in that it was a military court led by the victorious powers, and not an international one, it is a

Nuremberg Tribunal 1945: setting the standards of personal culpability

their lives destroyed. In former Yugoslavia, nearly four million people made refugees, 3-400,000 dead, perhaps as many as 100,000 women raped.

To dismiss the work of the International Tribunals on the basis of these absurd figures is unfair. There have never, before today, been international trials such as these for 'genocide' — Nuremberg was for 'crimes against humanity' — and this fact alone makes them crucial, even if the chances of bringing to trial the major architects of 'ethnic cleansing',

necessary reminder that World War II did not see, as people hoped, an end to genocidal practices. Beyond this, lawyers agree, the trial, if properly conducted, funded and organised, could have a potent symbolic value, particularly if seriously and widely reported; for a surfeit of horror, causing people to turn away, has become a new form of self-censorship. There is a provision, under the Tribunal's statutes, for trials of people who are not present to take the form of a public hearing at which the evidence is produced before a judge.

CAROLINE MOOREHEAD

IMPERIAL WAR MUSEUM

Changi jail, Singapore, March 1946: execution of a Japanese war criminal

has been issued for Nikolic's arrest.

How much people branded as mass murderers may actually suffer from the international opprobrium is impossible to gauge, but the message to other would-be murderers is plain: that the world is not prepared to sit by and let such crimes go unremarked, and that killers are not guaranteed automatic impunity. It is a message about the upholding of certain minimum rules about humanity and warfare, even if other notorious murderers — Siad Barre of Somalia, Baby Doc Duvalier of Haiti, Pol Pot of Cambodia, Idi Amin of Uganda and Saddam Hussein of Iraq — remain unpunished.

It is also, as the international lawyer Françoise Hampsen puts it, about reconciliation, and truth, and justice being seen if not to be done at least to be desired, without which a fresh start and a return of peace to places which have witnessed the horrors of Bosnia and Rwanda is impossible to envisage. 'Without truth,' said Judge Goldstone in a recent interview, 'especially where there have been serious human rights atrocities, there cannot be any enduring peace or any reconciliation.' ❑

One hearing has already taken place, and a Serbian camp commander called Dragan Nikolic has been found guilty of murder, torture, degrading and humiliating treatment. Once a suspect is pronounced guilty, the judge can sign an international arrest warrant with Interpol, when the indicted becomes the prisoner of the country in which he is sheltering, while the country itself is laid open to sanctioning measures. A warrant

Ariel Dorfman (2nd from left) with Jeremy Irons, Sinead Cusack and their son Sam

Death and the Maiden

It was particularly fitting, as the publishers of the first English-language version of the play at a time when its Chilean author, Ariel Dorfman, was living in forced exile, that *Index*/Writers & Scholars Educational Trust should have hosted the film première of *Death and the Maiden*. The evening at London's Curzon West End cinema on 19 April was a glittering occasion. The presence of the author drew out the stars as well as representatives from the theatre, the cinema and the media world. For those in the audience who had personal experience of Chilean brutality under the dictator, the evening was a moving as well as enjoyable occasion.

The event raised £10,000 for the continuing work of *Index*/WSET in those countries where oppression continues. *Index* would like to thank all who supported the première. ❏

Reader survey
It's now a year since our relaunch. We've had warm responses to the new **Index** from friends and the press. But, we want to know what you — the subscriber — have to say; please take five minutes to complete the reader survey enclosed with this issue.

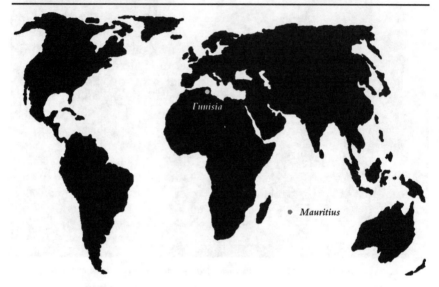

Tunisia

● *Mauritius*

Laws and the outlaw

'It's a question of principle. We have a duty to our readers.' So says Namassiwayam Ramalingum, editor-in-chief of the Mauritian weekly *L'Indépendant*, referring to his intention to return home and face down the Islamist militants who have firebombed his paper, threatened staff members and their families, and threatened him with death. Regardless of their lack of authority in the case of a non-believer, the mullahs have followed the fashionable practice of issuing a *fatwa* against him.

The purported cause of the campaign against *L'Indépendant* is an article it published about the prophet Mohammed, which militants claim offended the island's Muslim community. But there are deeper causes, altogether more mundane.

Since its launch in July 1993, *L'Indépendant* has been assiduous in rooting out corruption in high places. Success in exposing fraud has been matched by commercial success: the paper's circulation has grown fivefold in the last 18 months. Ramalingum has made some powerful enemies among government, opposition, big business and the media. It is these groups, Ramalingum believes, that are orchestrating Muslim support against his paper. The fact that the article in question was first published in *Le Point* and circulated in Algeria without incident appears to give the lie to any claim about offending religious sensibilities.

Not surprisingly, the authorities are falling over themselves to be unhelpful to Ramalingum: no official statements from President or prime minister denouncing the *fatwa* as an illegal act of incitement; no arrests of the individuals who publicly issued it. Instead, a message from the chief of police, warning Ramalingum to stay away from the country for a couple of weeks, because his safety cannot be guaranteed; while the Mauritian High Commissioner in London telephones journalists to tell them that the whole story is a fabrication on Ramalingum's part.

The government's lack of response to the threats made by Hindu fundamentalists against novelist Lindsey Collen (*Index* 4&5/1994) has already demonstrated its indifference towards the rule of law, and given the bully boys of whatever creed the green light. As Ramalingum said in May, 'They're going further and further because they think there's no political will to apply the law. It's getting more dangerous, not less.'

Tunisian journalists, on the other hand, are stifling under a surfeit of laws that regulate their profession: journalists must not write anything that defames the President or any official body; must not 'defame public order'; must not spread or reproduce 'false information'; and on and on.

Reporters have lived with the regulations so long they have become adept at complying with them: self-censorship is the rule. The fact that Tunisian journalists appear relatively rarely in these pages is itself an index of unfreedom in that country, an ominous silence that betokens their subjugation.

Now a group of the country's most senior journalists have had enough. A letter circulated in April, courageously signed by leading members of the Tunisian Association of Journalists (whose names, for their own protection, must go unpublished here), criticises that organisation for its eagerness to go along with the Press Code, and cries out for a free union that can defend independent journalism rather than simply extending the government's reach into the very heart of the profession.

That, as Namassiwayam Ramalingum would say, is a question of principle. ❏

Adam Newey

A censorship chronicle incorporating information from the American Association for the Advancement of Science Human Rights Action Network (AAASHRAN), Amnesty International (AI), Article 19 (A19), the BBC Monitoring Service Summary of World Broadcasts (SWB), the Central American Centre for the Protection of Freedom of Expression (CEPEX), the Committee to Protect Journalists (CPJ), the Canadian Committee to Protect Journalists (CCPJ), the International Federation of Journalists (IFJ/FIP), Human Rights Watch (HRW), the Media Institute of Southern Africa (MISA), International PEN (PEN), Open Media Research Institute Daily Digest (OMRI), Reporters Sans Frontières (RSF), the West African Journalists' Association (UJAO) and other sources.

AFGHANISTAN

Behroze Khan, a Pakistani journalist with United Press International and president of the Peshawar Press Club, and Ian Steward, an American journalist with UPI, were arrested outside the Intercontinental Hotel in Kabul on 24 March. The authorities claimed that the two did not have legal travel documents. (Pakistan Press Foundation)

Recent publications: *The Human Rights Crisis and the Refugees* (AI, February 1995, 13pp); *Executions, Amputations and Possible Deliberate and Arbitrary Killings* (AI, April 1995, 6pp); *Women in Afghanistan: A Human Rights*

Catastrophe (AI, May 1995, 15pp)

ALBANIA

Agim Bendo, chief justice of Tirana's district court, and his deputies resigned on 31 March, accusing justice minister Hektor Frasheri of trying to bring the court under his Ministry's jurisdiction, of trying to prevent the hearing of cases and of attempting to influence the hiring and firing of employees. (OMRI)

On 4 April the Association of Journalists called on the government to lift customs duties on newsprint, the circulation tariff on newspapers and tax on advertisements, and to exempt the Demokracia printing house from tax and duty, saying that high production costs are a threat to press freedom and democracy (*Index* 4&5/1994). (SWB)

Ilir Hoxha, son of ex-dictator Enver Hoxha, was placed under house arrest on 18 April because of views he expressed in an interview with the paper *Modeste*. He is charged with 'endangering public peace by inciting hatred between sections of the population and by slandering them'. If convicted he could face up to five years in prison under the defamation law. (Reuter)

Perparim Xhihxa, former editor of Socialist Party daily *Zeri i Popullit*, was placed under house arrest on 20 April in connection with the disappearance of funds in 1991 from a Communist solidarity fund, which were allegedly

used to pay for printing equipment. (OMRI)

May Day celebrations planned by the Confederation of Trade Unions in Tirana were banned by police, who said that they might endanger public order and disrupt traffic. Only private meetings outside the city were reported to have been allowed. (OMRI)

ALGERIA

The murder of journalists continues: Mohammed Abderrahmani, editor-in-chief of the government daily *El Moudjahid*, was killed on 27 March in Oued Kniss; ENTV reporter Rachida Hammadi died on 30 March from wounds received in a gun attack in which her sister Houria, a secretary also with ENTV, died 10 days before. The Armed Islamic Group (GIA) claimed responsibility for the sisters' murders. Makhlouf Boukhezar, an ENTV journalist, had his throat cut during the night of 3-4 April by attackers who posed as police officers to gain entry to his home in Constantine. (CPJ, RSF)

Ali Boukerbache, owner of a private television production company, Media–TV, was shot dead on 21 March. He had previously been a journalist with *El Djoumhouria*. (CPJ)

Abdelkader Hadj Benaamane, Tamanrasset correspondent for the state news agency APS, was arrested in April and is being detained without charge, apparently in connection with an internal wire written by the journalist which mentioned FIS leaders. (RSF)

ARGENTINA

Former naval officer Captain Adolfo Francisco Scilingo said, in an article published on 3 March by the daily paper *Página 12*, that up to 2,000 political prisoners were thrown into the ocean from navy aircraft during the military dictatorship (1976-83). President Menem, however, has urged those responsible for atrocities 'not to rub salt in the wounds' by talking about them. (*El País, Independent*)

On 22 March Maria Alejandra Bonafini, daughter of Hebe Bonafini, the president of the Mothers of the Plaza de Mayo, received an anonymous death threat. The incident is believed to be connected to her mother's declarations on human rights in the context of new admissions made by army officials relating to disappearances during the dictatorship. (AI)

Dozens of human rights activists were injured in clashes with police, who used water cannons to break up a demonstration outside the Mechanics School, a torture centre during the military dictatorship. The demonstrators were demanding a list of military personnel responsible for human rights violations. (Reuter)

ARMENIA

Journalists called an end to

their protests against the closure of opposition papers (*Index* 2/1995) on 3 March, despite the government's failure to allow the papers to reopen. (SWB)

AUSTRALIA

A 30 April report on the Australian Secret Intelligence Service (ASIS) recommended increased sanctions against civil servants and journalists who expose illegal activity by state agencies. If leaked information is from current intelligence operations, the proposed changes will rule out any public interest defence. Those convicted of breaking the new law could be liable to seven years' imprisonment. The recommendations would be enacted in two stages. Initially, only public servants would be affected; the media would be expected to censor themselves if authorities label a story with a 'D' notice. Only if self-censorship fails would the government employ the new law against journalists. (*Melbourne Sunday Age*, Reuter)

AZERBAIJAN

On 17 March Reuters cameraman Adil Bunyatov was killed while filming an attack by Azeri government troops on the headquarters of a rebel police unit on the outskirts of Baku. (CPJ)

Four journalists were detained on 24 March for their alleged part in the publication and distribution of a newspaper, *Cheshmah*, which carried articles deemed to be defamatory

to President Aliyev. The four — Yadigar Mamedli, editor of the opposition paper *Jumhuriyet*, Malik Bayramov, who works for the opposition People's Front press service, Ayaz Ahmedov of the the ANI news agency and Asker Ahmed, member of the Musavat party — face up to six years in prison if convicted. The editors-in-chief of 14 independent newspapers announced a week-long strike on 27 March to protest what they see as increasing political censorship by the special department of the president's office, the Baku commandant's office, and Glavlit, the state censorship office. (CPJ, SWB)

The pro-People's Front paper *Azadlya* failed to appear three times between 17 and 26 March, because censors demanded the deletion of several articles on the police mutiny of 17 March. The editors said that, under such circumstances, they preferred not to produce the paper at all. (SWB)

BAHRAIN

Security forces used tear gas and live ammunition to break up a student pro-democracy strike at Duraz intermediate school on 25 March, killing Hamid Abdulla Y Qassim and severely injuring several others (*Index* 1/1995). (Bahrain Human Rights Organisation)

Sheikh Abd al-Amir al-Jamri, a prominent Shi'a Muslim scholar who has frequently called for the reinstatement of parliament, was placed under

'Belarusian journalist... Belarusian typewriter.'

RSF

house arrest together with 18 members of his family on 1 April. His detention sparked protests in the village of Bani Jamra. Security forces responded with live ammunition, killing two men — Muhammad Ja'far Yusuf Atiyya and Muhammad Ali Abd al-Razzaq — and seriously wounding others. On 15 April al-Jamri was removed by police to an unspecified location. (AI)

BANGLADESH

Leaders of the opposition Awami League claimed on 9 March that the government had arrested nearly 100 anti-government activists in an attempt to forestall a nationwide strike planned for 12-13 March. (Reuter)

Islamists demanded the hanging of parliamentarian Farida Rahman at the end of March,

after she said that women should have equal property rights with men. The leader of the Combined Islamic Action Council, Fazlul Huq Amini, said he would continue to put pressure on the government to hang Rehman, as he had done for Taslima Nasrin. (*Times*)

A reception in honour of the poet Shamsur Rahman, due to be held in Sylhet on 18 April, had to be cancelled after Islamists, believed to belong to Jamaat-e-Islami, ransacked the venue. Rahman is considered an apostate by Islamist groups. (SWB)

BELARUS

On 17 March President Lukasenka dismissed Iosif Seredich, editor of the paper *Narodnaya Gazeta* and a parliamentary deputy, for publishing a letter that criticised

Lukasenka's pro-Russian policies, on the grounds that the letter 'incited violence and civil unrest'. (CPJ)

On 12 April troops entered Parliament and forcibly evicted deputies who were staging a sit-in and hunger strike to protest against President Lukasenka's plans to hold a national referendum on establishing closer ties with Russia. (SWB)

All discussion of election issues was barred on national broadcast media prior to the elections and referendum which were held on 14 May. Only local stations were allowed to follow the campaign. The current affairs television programme *Prospect* was also prevented by the President's press secretary from showing interviews with the Polish and US ambassadors on 14 May and has since been cancelled. (*Minsk Economic News*)

BOLIVIA

A meeting of the Bolivian Workers' Central (COB) was broken up by police with rubber bullets on 18 April. Several journalists who filmed the incident were assaulted and had their equipment confiscated. Sixteen of them were arrested and taken to the border with Chile and seven remain in detention. On the night of 18 April the government declared a state of emergency and assumed emergency powers allowing the security forces to keep anyone in detention for an unlimited period without charge. In the southern province of Tarija, a group of citizens declared administrative independence from the government of President Gonzalo Sánchez de Lozada, in the face of general unrest in the country. (Reuter, RSF)

BOSNIA-HERCEGOVINA

Amir Talic, a poet and leader of the Muslim humanitarian organisation Merhamet who was abducted by Bosnian Serb forces on 22 February, is being held on unspecified charges in Tunjice prison in Banja Luca, along with other leaders of the organisation. (Reuter, PEN)

Bosnian Muslim novelist Bajram Redzepagic, who had been held by military authorities in Sarajevo since 28 February on charges of helping someone avoid military service, was released pending trial on 14 March. He allegedly received injuries in custody. Redzepagic is a well known critic of the government. (AI, PEN)

Journalists Namik Berberovic and Shanaat Nahrawand (*Index* 2/1995) were freed on 20 March by Bosnian Serb forces as part of a prisoner exchange. (CPJ, RSF)

UNPROFOR began issuing a single accreditation card to both local and foreign journalists on 1 May. Previously, two different types of press card had been issued to reporters, which, it was argued, made it easy for paramilitary forces to identify local journalists. (CPJ)

BOTSWANA

Charges of leaking secrets against two journalists with the weekly *Mmegi* have been dismissed. Managing editor Titus Mbuya and freelance reporter Professor Malema, were accused of publishing classified information in the early 1990s, outlining news on workers' demands made during a general strike. The ruling is unlikely to set a precedent on issues of official secrecy, however, as the National Security Act gives the government sweeping powers to withhold information. (MISA)

BURMA

Recent publication: *Censorship Prevails: Political Deadlock and Economic Transition in Burma* (A19, March 1995, 45pp)

BURUNDI

Journalists and aid workers claim to have been prevented by the police and army from investigating scenes of Tutsi massacres of Hutus. Amnesty International delegates also say that the army chief, Colonel Jean Bikomagu, denied access to areas of army action against Hutu militias in Kanyosha, after reports of hundreds of civilians' bodies lining the roads in late March. (AI, *Independent*)

A radical Tutsi newspaper, *La Nation*, owned by Burundi's former dictator, Jean-Baptiste Bagaza, has been backing the Tutsi militias that have been terrorising Hutu neighbourhoods, it was reported in

April. The newspaper calls for the murder of opponents and foreign diplomats, including the US and UN ambassadors. (*Guardian*)

South African journalist Francis Vincent and his unnamed Burundian interpreter were killed in an ambush near Bujumbura on 6 April. A Burundian driver later died of his injuries. Hutu militias are believed to be responsible for the attack, in which a cameraman was also injured. (RSF)

Recent publication: *Breaking the Cycle of Violence*, by Filip Reyntjens (Minority Rights Group, 1995, 30pp)

CAMBODIA

Foreign minister Ung Huot said on 4 May that the UN Human Rights Centre would be allowed to remain in the country. The government had previously threatened to close the Centre because its reports were detrimental to the country's image. Ung said that Phnom Penh would be happy for the Centre to remain, albeit with certain changes to its mandate. (AFP)

CAMEROON

On 22 March armed police surrounded the headquarters of the opposition Union of Democratic Forces (UFDC) in Yaounde, to prevent dissident writer Mongo Beti addressing a meeting to discuss his new book, *France against Africa*, an attack on French development aid to its former colonies. (Reuter)

On 17 April two newspaper vendors were arrested, and another manhandled by police, for selling that day's edition of *Le Messager*, which contained an article critical of Vice-President Andz Tsoungui. (A19)

CHINA

Two newspapers, *Hsien Tai Jih Pao*, and the English-language *Hong Kong News*, were closed and forced to cease printing in Beijing in January. A Beijing-based paper for the disabled, *Xinshenhuo Bao*, is reported to have been 'under scrutiny' for operating an illegal recruitment policy. (SWB)

Gu Jieshu was executed in Beijing on 24 February for producing and selling pornographic books. Seven others received jail sentences for similar offences. (SWB)

Detained dissident Wei Jinsheng (*Index* 7/1992, 6/1994) has been nominated for the Nobel peace prize. A Foreign Ministry spokesman described the detained activist as a criminal, and said 'he has no qualification whatsoever to be nominated for the so-called Nobel peace prize.' Fears for Wei's health have grown following the Foreign Ministry's refusal to say where he is being held, or even confirm that he is still alive. (RSF)

The Chinese Film Administration said on 18 April that it will abandon quotas on foreign film imports and will fulfill its promise to import 'the 10 most popular films' each year. However,

the Administration will continue to make sure imported films are 'in line with the Chinese situation and laws'. (SWB)

Recent publications: *Death Penalty Log: July to December 1994* (AI, March 1995, 28pp); *Trade Unionism in China: A Ban on Pluralism* (AI, May 1995, 6pp)

COLOMBIA

Members of the Civic Human Rights Committee of Meta based in Villavicencio received death threats on 15 March. The Committee assists families displaced as a result of army and guerrilla activity in the Ariari region, and reports on human rights violations by the army and their paramilitary allies, including the group known as 'Black Snake'. In recent weeks, harassment and intimidation directed at Committee members has increased significantly. (AI)

Wilson José Cáceres González, a founding member of the Civic Movement of Sabana de Torres, and a mayoral candidate for the Worker and Popular Peasant Farmer Movement, is reported to have disappeared on 6 April, on his way home from work. (AI)

On 6 April Richard Freddy Muñoz, Cali correspondent for the national television news programme *QAP*, received an anonymous phone call ordering him to leave Cali within three days. Muñoz left the following day, with cameraman Diego Balanta.

Gregorio Perez of the television news programme *Hoy*, and Humberto Briñez and Embert Charam of *CMI* also left Cali after similar threats. In Valledupar Lolita Acosta Maestre, publisher of the daily paper *Diario Vallenato*, escaped an assassination attempt on 6 April. The incidents are believed to be related to the journalists' reporting of arrests of Cali drug cartel members. (CPJ)

On 11 April President Samper issued a statement in which he declared his commitment to freedom of the press, and announced an investigation into the recent threats against journalists. The leaders of the Cali drug cartel denied any involvement in intimidating and threatening journalists, in a statement in the daily *El Espectador* on April 10. (CPJ, Reuter)

Recent publication: *Trade Unionists in Colombia: A Tenuous Grip on Life* (AI, May 1995, 5pp)

COTE D'IVOIRE

David Deliwa Gogbe (*Index* 3/1994, 1/1995), editor of the weekly *Le Changement*, was sentenced to six months in prison for libel on 15 March, in connection with a letter published by the paper in January. (Radio France Internationale)

On 20 March *La Patrie* journalist De Be Kwassi (*Index* 2/1995) began a hunger strike to protest his one-year sentence for offending the head of state. On 30 March he was admitted to hospital, and has since started eating again. On 12 April the Court of Appeal rejected Kwassi's request for conditional release. (Reuter, SWB)

CROATIA

On 22 March Parliament voted to cancel live media coverage of its proceedings. Opposition parties criticised the Speaker for procedural violations in the conduct of the vote and for refusing to repeat the vote after a mistake in counting the number of deputies opposed. (SWB)

Mirko Buzak, an international women's aid convoy representative, was detained by Serb forces in the Serb enclave of Krajina at the end of March. UN peacekeeping officers in Knin were prevented from visiting him in custody. The convoy, carrying food and medicine bound for Bihac, had been held up for five days when Krajina Serbs refused it passage. (Reuter)

In late March the Constitutional Court exempted the satirical weekly *Feral Tribune* from the 50 per cent sales tax levied on pornographic publications, which was imposed on it in July 1994 (*Index* 4&5/1994). *Feral Tribune* regularly criticises and satirises President Tudjman. The tax had forced the paper to the brink of bankruptcy. (AIM, Agence Europe)

A military court in Krajina sentenced Bendif Oliver Slemen, a French journalist, to two-and-a-half years in prison on 12 April, for entering the enclave illegally. (SWB)

CUBA

On 2 March Néstor Baguer, (*Index* 10/1992) president of the unofficial Association of Independent Cuban Journalists (APIC), was attacked by an unknown individual outside his home in Havana. The assailant pushed him off the pavement into the street, causing a fracture to his right wrist and severe bruising to his ribs. The attack occurred a few days after Baguer was to attend a function to mark the opening of a book exhibition organised by the American Association of Publishers. Several other people reported having difficulty getting in to the event, either because their invitations were unexpectedly cancelled, or they were refused entry at the door. (APIC)

CYPRUS

On 16 March the Medical Council declared Theocharis Theokli Theocharidis (*Index* 2/1995) unfit for military exercises on health grounds, thereby exempting him from military service. (AI)

CZECH REPUBLIC

A court in Kromeriz sentenced Zdeneck Svarovsky to four months in jail, suspended for one year, on 16 March, after he was found guilty of defaming President Havel. A spokesman said that Havel would not comment on the case. (OMRI)

Members of the pop group Branik were given an eight-month suspended sentence on 25 April, after the lyrics of their songs were found to be 'racially defamatory'. (SWB)

EGYPT

Angela Stephens, an American journalist, and Lorraine Chitock, a British journalist, were arrested on 11 March and held for five days after attempting to enter Egypt via desert routes from Sudan. The journalists claimed that they had been researching traditional camel journeys made by Sudanese camel traders. The main border crossing between Sudan and Egypt is closed for security reasons. (Reuter)

The four-month ban on Youssef Chahine's film *al-Muhajer* (The Emigrant) (*Index* 1/1995, 2/1995) was lifted by a Cairo court on 29 March. (*Guardian*)

ETHIOPIA

Asrat Woldeyes (*Index* 6/1994), leader of the All-Amhara People's Organisation, was sentenced to a further six months in prison for contempt of court after he said that he 'had no hope of a fair trial'. In December 1994 he was sentenced to three years for incitement against the government. (AAASHRAN)

Andarge Mesfin and Tekle Mesfin, reporters with the weekly *Tenager*, were reportedly sentenced to 18 months and one year respectively on 24 March, for publishing a communiqué from the Oromo Liberation Front and several other political documents. Both are appealing the sentences. (PEN)

Despite international pressure, the main opposition parties are expected to boycott the May elections for the 'ethnic federal' constitution, to succeed the four-year Transitional Government. The Southern Ethiopian People's Democratic Coalition (SEPDC) pulled out after the ruling Ethiopian People's Revolutionary Democratic Front released only 90 of over 300 SEPDC detainees, and refused guarantees of security, election funding and open electioneering to the opposition. Although the government has promised open access to state-run media, it has used laws against the dissemination of false information to encourage self-censorship. (*Africa Confidential*)

Recent publication: *Accountability Past and Present — Human Rights in Transition* (AI, April 1995, 58pp)

FRANCE

The Paris High Court issued an order in early April banning the distribution of the Christian Communities Bible. The bible, a simplified version of the Old and New Testaments, was banned for two passages which were deemed to be anti-Semitic. (*International Herald Tribune*)

On 27 April the European Court of Human Rights ruled

in favour of Dorothée Piermont, a member of the European Parliament, who was expelled from French Polynesia and barred from entering New Caledonia after she addressed an anti-nuclear protest during a parliamentary campaign in 1986. The Court ordered France to pay 80,000 francs to cover legal costs. (*International Herald Tribune*)

On 2 May 1995 interior minister Charles Pasqua banned a book of Islamic theology, *The Permissible and the Impermissible in Islam*, on the grounds that it endangered public order. The book, written by Youssef Qaradhawi, has been available in France since 1992. (*Independent*)

GABON

The offices of the paper *L'Effort Gabonais* were sealed off by security forces on 14 March, bypassing the usual procedure for suspending publications, which is the province of the National Communications Council (CNC). A request from the interior minister for a temporary ban on the paper was still being considered by the CNC when the security forces were sent in. (SWB)

On 20 April the interior minister ordered the national printing press to cease printing the papers *Le Bucheron* and *La Griffe*. Both had reprinted articles from the French press, referring to the case against an Italian tailor currently on trial in France for setting up a prostitution ring, whose clients are alleged to have

included President Bongo. The National Communications Council overturned the ban five days later and the papers have resumed publication. (Reuter)

GAMBIA

Pap Saine, director of the weekly *Le Point*, and two journalists, Badara Sowe and Brima Ernest, were arrested on 30 March following the publication of a series of articles about a riot in the central prison in Banjul. (RSF, Reuter, UJAO)

GREECE

On 16 March the Athens-based private television station, Mega TV, was extensively damaged by a rocket-grenade attack. No injuries were reported. The left-wing guerrilla group November 17 claimed responsibility for the attack. (Reuter, SWB)

On 28 April President Costis Stephanopoulos accused Macedonia of claiming the entire Macedonian region, which includes areas in Greece and Bulgaria, because of its refusal to remove an ancient Greek symbol from its flag. (Reuter)

GUATEMALA

After a three-year campaign, US citizen Jennifer Harbury was officially informed by US congressman Robert Torricelli of the death of her husband, URNG combatant Efraín Bámaca Velásquez, who was captured on 12 March 1992.

In a 22 March letter to President Clinton, Torricelli disclosed evidence that Bámaca's death and that of US citizen Michael Devine had been ordered by Colonel Julio Roberto Alpírez, a former CIA employee. The CIA had blocked the release of this information. President Clinton fired the CIA station chief in Guatemala and announced that he would punish any individual involved in concealing information on the case. The State Department also announced the suspension of military aid to Guatemala. (*Mesoamerica*)

Gerson López Orantes, a journalist with *La República*, was abducted in Guatemala City on 28 March by unidentified assailants and tortured and interrogated about his investigations into Noel de Jesus, accused of the murder of the anthropologist Myrna Mack Chang (*Index* 3/1992, 4/1993), Ricardo Ortega, who is accused of killing a young girl, and an army officer who is allegedly involved in the drugs trade and the sale of stolen vehicles. López was released the next day and given 72 hours to leave the country. (FIP)

The home of *Prensa Libre* journalist Jorge Mazariegos de León was burgled on 5 April and a telephone book and notebooks stolen. He has been investigating cases of military officers reputed to be on the CIA payroll. A week earlier documents and files were stolen from the home of Juan Guadenzi, a correspondent for the Mexican daily *Reforma* and

consultant to the UN Mission for Guatemala (MINAGUA). (CEPEX)

On 12 April in the US District Court, Boston, eight Guatemalans and a US nun, Sister Dianna Ortiz (*Index* 3/1990), were awarded damages of US$47,000,000 for human rights abuses committed by Guatemala's former defence minister General Gramajo, who is currently running for president. The cases were brought while Gramajo was studying at Harvard University's Kennedy School of Government in 1991 (*Index* 2/1992). (Reuter)

Juan Emilio Colmenares, director of the station Radio Mopán in El Petén, reported in early May that members of the army and police have

made frequent threats to occupy and destroy the station. Colmenares believes the threats are connected with allegations of corruption the station has made against a local judge. (CEPEX)

On 7 May the daily *Siglo XXI* reported that staff members had received telephone threats over the previous three days, telling them not to continue investigating stories that are 'none of their concern'. Some observers believe the threats relate to the paper's investigations into human rights abuses committed by the military. (CEPEX, FIP)

Recent publication: *Disappeared in Guatemala: The Case of Efraín Bámaca Velásquez* (HRW/Americas, March 1995, 15pp)

GUINEA-BISSAU

João de Barros, editor-in-chief of the weekly *Correio da Guine-Bissau*, was arrested and beaten at the Bissau airport as he was waiting to board a plane to Cape Verde on 8 March. The officers who detained him claimed that he did not have permission to leave the country, but had no written documentation to this effect. (RSF)

HAITI

Carl Maris Loisseau, a member of the organisation Mouvman Jen Aveni Popla, was arrested by US troops while putting up anti-American posters in Port-au-Prince on 20 March. He was beaten by US and Haitian soldiers and released three days later. (*Haiti Info*)

On 23 March three journalists and a cameraman were assaulted by the Presidential Guard while filming members of the Guard beating an unidentified man. (RSF)

Recent publication: *Security Compromised: 'Recycled' Haitian Soldiers on the Police Front Line* (HRW/Americas, March 1995, 26pp)

HONDURAS

It was reported in April that army officers Colonel Juan Blas Salazar, Colonel Juan César Fuñez, Major Manuel Trejo and retired Lieutenant Jordi Montanola are to stand trial in civilian courts for the disappearance of 184 people in the 1980s. (*Mesoamerica*)

HONG KONG

Police raided the offices of seven of Hong Kong's eight internet providers on 3 March, rendering subscribers all over the colony unable to log on. The reason for the raid is unclear. (*Guardian*)

The colony's leading Communist journal, *Contemporary*, is set to close for financial reasons. The closure of the journal, often critical of Chinese prime minister Li Peng, and in other matters generally regarded as unbiased, is the latest in a series of setbacks to press freedom in the run-up to Chinese rule in 1997. (*Times*)

HUNGARY

The state holding company AV Rt dismissed Peter Molnar, the managing director of newspaper publisher Hirlapkiado Rt, on 8 April. Privatisation minister Tamas Schuman has also initiated disciplinary proceedings against Molnar for his sacking of Attila O Kovacs, editor of *Esti Hirlap*, after the paper published reports damaging to AV Rt. *Esti Hirlap* appeared with a blank page on 1 April after Molnar had removed several reports about the editor's dismissal. (Reuter, *Heti Vilaggazdasag*)

The journalists' union issued a statement on 14 April, saying that the dismissal of at least 1,000 Hungarian TV staff this year is unconstitutional and asking Parliament to launch an appeal to the Constitutional Court. (SWB)

INDIA

Since January, the Calcutta police department has charged four drama troupes with obscenity. Their shows, with titles such as *The Raped* and *Poisonous Kiss*, show passionate kissing between men and women. A police spokesman said the plays fuel depravity. (*International Herald Tribune*)

Journalists walked out of a press conference in Cuttack on 8 March in protest at the Election Commission's refusal to grant press passes to all who applied to cover the district elections. Of the eight passes which were issued, five went to the official media, and the rest to a single newspaper. (*Asian Age*)

The town of Charar-e-Sharief in Jammu and Kashmir state was declared out of bounds to the media by military authorities on 20 March. The army were besieging militants occupying the town, who had refused an offer of safe passage to Azad Kashmir. (*Tribune*)

Fifteen journalists were injured, five seriously, in Jammu on 31 March when police broke up a peaceful protest organised by the Jammu Journalists' Association against police attacks on reporters. Among the injured were Sujay Mehdudia of United News of India, SMA Kazmi of *Indian Express*, Shakeel Akhtar of *Navbharat Times*, MK Bangroo of Press Trust of India, Ved Bhasin and Parmod Jamwal of *Kashmir Times*, Imrana Samani, editor of *Sandesh*,

Anuradha Bhasin editor-in-chief of *Springer* and Harbans Nagoke of *Danik Jagran*. (*Tribune*)

Following the election of an extremist Hindu leadership in the state of Maharashtra, police in Bombay started to round up Muslim settlers from Pakistan and Bangladesh at the end of March. Bal Thackeray, leader of Shiv Sena and de facto leader of the state government, has threatened to purge the entire country of Muslims. (*Times*)

Nearly 35,000 activists from opposition parties were arrested across Tamil Nadu state on 4 May. They had organised a strike to reinforce demands that chief minister Jayalalitha Jayaram resign. Jayaram is currently under investigation for corruption. (*International Herald Tribune*)

Recent publications: *Human Rights in Kashmir: Report of a Mission* (International Commission of Jurists, 1995, 140 pp); *Analysis of the Government of India's Response to Amnesty International's Report on Jammu and Kashmir* (AI, March 1995, 38pp)

INDONESIA

Two activists from the Jakarta-based organisation Pijar were arrested on 10 March for 'public expression of hostility or contempt against state institutions'. The arrest of Tri Agus Susanto and Syahrul is believed to be linked to Pijar's independent publication *Kabar dari Pijar*, which is often critical of the

government. (AI, Tapol)

On 28 March the government asked editors of several papers to dismiss 45 journalists for belonging to the unofficial Alliance of Independent Journalists (AJI) (*Index* 4&5/1994, 6/1994). According to reports some editors have, under government pressure, blackmailed several staff reporters, forcing them to either leave the AJI or resign their jobs. Thirteen AJI members were formally expelled from the official Indonesian Journalists' Association (PWI) on 17 March. By law, all journalists must belong to the PWI. (RSF, SWB)

Three members of the AJI are to face trial for 'sowing hatred against the government', their lawyer announced on 17 April. AJI general secretary Ahmad Taufik, Eko Maryadi and Danang Wardoyo are also charged with illegally distributing *Indepens*, the AJI's underground paper. The three, detained on 16 March, face up to seven years in prison if convicted. (Reuter, AI, Tapol)

The latest book by dissident writer Pramoedya Ananta Toer (*Index* 5/1981, 4/1986, 3,1990), entitled *Silent Song of a Dumb Man*, was banned by order of the attorney-general on 19 April. The order said that the book, a series of essays recounting Pramoedya's 10 years in a hard labour penal colony on Buru island, 'contains distortions that could create erroneous opinions about the government... and

its continued circulation might cause unrest and disturb public order.' (Tapol)

George Aditjondro (*Index* 6/1994) is likely to face trial for insulting the government, his lawyer said on 22 April. Aditjondro, prominent for his criticism of Jakarta's East Timor policies, was questioned by police last October for remarks he made at a seminar. Aditjondro is currently teaching in Australia and it is not clear whether he will return to Indonesia. (Reuter)

Around 19 students and labourers were arrested in Jakarta and Semarang on 1 May for staging wage protests. Five of the detainees, who were released the next day, plan to lodge formal complaints with the National Human Rights Commission. The protests for higher wages, the first this year, attracted up to 500 people across central Java. (Reuter)

The ban on *Tempo* (*Index* 4&5/1994) was unexpectedly overturned by the Jakarta Administrative Court on 3 May. Ruling that the ban contravenes the National Press Law which forbids censorship, the court ordered that *Tempo*'s publishing licence be restored. The court also ruled in favour of a suit by former *Tempo* employees against information minister Harmoko for the loss of their jobs. Harmoko said the government would appeal both decisions. (*International Herald Tribune*, *Financial Times*)

Recent publications: *Attacks*

on *Free Speech* (AI, April 1995, 7pp); *Trade Unionists in Indonesia* (AI, May 1995, 7pp)

IRAN

Retired General Azizollah Amir Rahimi (*Index* 1/1995) was released from prison on 12 March. His son, Mehrdad Amir Rahimi, had been freed on bail on 1 March. Press reports say General Rahimi was released 'for health reasons'. (*Guardian*)

The government banned the literary magazine *Takapoo* in mid-March after it published the open letter about freedom of expression signed by 134 writers (*Index* 6/1994, p63), an article about the letter entitled 'Literature and Power', and a poem by Reza Baraheni, which has been described by the authorities as 'promotion of decadence and prostitution'. (Iranian Writers in Exile)

An Islamic Human Rights Commission came into being on 21 March with the aim of defining, defending and promoting an Islamic conception of human rights. Although primarily a domestic institution, the Commission will also pay attention to the global protection of Islamic human rights. It will be led by Ayatollah Yazdi, who also heads the judiciary in Iran. (SWB)

Around 10 people were shot and hundreds more arrested by the Revolutionary Guard during demonstrations in the Tehran suburb of Islamshahr on 4 April. The demonstra-

tions reportedly started as a march by about 200 youths in protest against bus fare increases and poor water quality, but developed into a wider protest against economic hardship. (AI)

The law banning satellite dishes (*Index* 1/1995) came into force on 22 April. Official reports claim that 80 per cent of owners have dismantled their dishes voluntarily. (SWB)

ISRAEL

Abdul Karim Khabeisa, cameraman for Worldwide Television News, was arrested by defence forces in February allegedly for inciting youths to throw stones in Nablus. WTN bureau chief Chris Slaney denied the allegations and claimed that Abdul Karim had been threatened by Israeli authorities twice before. (*Guardian*)

On 14 March the attorney-general asked the police to examine the contents of *Baruch, The Man*, a book eulogising Baruch Goldstein, the Kiryat Arba settler responsible for the Dome of the Rock massacre in February 1994. The 533-page book, which has sold thousands of copies, could be banned on the grounds that it incites violence against Arabs. (*Times*)

Nadjii Dana, cameraman with French television network TF1, was arrested by Israeli soldiers on 19 March while filming after the murders of two settlers near Hebron. Nahum Varnea, journalist

with the daily *Yedioth Ahronot*, was attacked on 20 March by angry demonstrators while covering the settlers' funerals near Hebron. Another settler came to Varnea's rescue when nearby police refused to intervene to help him. (RSF)

Several journalists were attacked by soldiers following the 9 April car bombings in Gaza. At least three were arrested and briefly detained: Shlomi Eldar of Israeli State Television, Najib Abu Djubein, cameraman with Associated Press, and Muhammad Daoudi, cameraman with WTN, who received a gunshot wound to the hand during the arrest. (RSF)

Nine students were arrested when soldiers raided student accommodation at Birzeit University in the early hours of 12 April. Books, magazines and study materials were confiscated. (*Jerusalem Times*)

The East Jerusalem printing press offices of Palestinian newspaper *al-Uma* were raided on 20 April and printing equipment removed by a group believed to be connected to the Palestinian Authority's security forces. (Reuter)

The military censor has allowed Israeli newspapers *Kol Ha'ir*, its associated regional papers owned by Shoken publishing group, and *Ha'aretz* to publish new revelations about the kidnapping of Mordechai Vanunu, convicted of treason in 1986 for leaking nuclear secrets and held in solitary confinement (*Index* 1/1987, 5/1988, 6/1994). (Reuter, *Sunday Times*)

Ofer Nimrodi and Arnon Mozes, publishers of the dailies *Ma'ariv* and *Yediot Aharanot* respectively, were taken into custody on 25 April and accused of wiretapping each other's offices, as well as those of senior politicians and business figures. Nimrodi was released on 28 April, but confined to his house. (*Independent, Guardian*)

Soldiers raided the Nablus Office for the Press in the West Bank on 8 May, confiscated news reports and publications, and sealed the premises in accordance with a six-month suspension order from the Israeli military commander. The Office, which serves as a news outlet for several Palestinian news organisations, is deemed to be distributing 'inciting material'. (CPJ)

Recent publication: *Making Education Illegal: Students from the Gaza Strip — Israeli Restrictions and International Reactions*, by Nigel Parry (Human Rights Action Project, January 1995, 42pp. From: Birzeit University, PO Box 14, Birzeit, West Bank, via Israel)

ITALY

The independent daily *La Voce* ceased publication on 12 March. The Milan-based paper, founded a year ago by Indro Montanelli (*Index* 4&5/1994, p25), has fallen victim to rising costs, falling readership, and a marketing war with more established daily papers. (*Guardian, Times*)

Recent publication: *Alleged Torture and Ill-Treatment by Law Enforcement and Prison Officers* (AI, April 1995, 23pp)

KAZAKHSTAN

The paper *Kazakhskaya Pravda* has been shut down for anti-Semitism and inciting ethnic hatred, it was reported on 6 April. There have been frequent demands for its closure over the past year. (*Izvestiya*)

Officials broke in to the printing works of the Pavlodar paper *Zvezda Priirtyshya* in mid-April, in an attempt to halt publication of an article criticising a referendum on the extension of President Nazarbayev's term of office to the year 2000. Most of the 40,000 print run had already been distributed, so the officials undertook a series of raids on the homes of subscribers, during which around 2,000 copies were confiscated. (*Nezavisimaya Gazeta*)

KENYA

Two reporters with the *Nation*, Alex Cege and Julius Mokaya, were dismissed in January shortly after the government threatened to ban the paper. Cege was sacked because of a story alleging a government minister had bought an office block at less than its market value. Mokaya was dismissed after he quoted lawyers who criticised the attorney-general as the main obstacle to rewriting the constitution. (A19)

The government has banned a Kikuyu-language diocesan newsletter, *Inooro*, it was reported in March. (*Sunday Nation*)

Opposition MP Linus Oluoch Polo was charged with sedition in March because of remarks he made about President Moi at a public gathering. (A19)

The offices of the legal aid centre Kituo Cha Seira and the Kenya Human Rights Commission were firebombed on 15 March, causing extensive damage. Two security guards were also shot in the attack. (AI)

The government has confiscated *Nuru*, the publication of the banned human rights and legal organisation Mwangaza Trust. On 4 April six opposition MPs were arrested at the Trust's offices for holding an illegal meeting, among them Paul Muite, the Ford-Kenya MP who heads the Trust and is the lawyer defending Koigi wa Wamwere (*Index* 6/1994); and Maina Wachira, head of the independent Institute of Economic Affairs. Gatherings of more than three people require a permit issued by a district or provincial commissioner. (A19, *Guardian, Ngao*)

Catholic church leaders, who criticised the government on 1 April for instigating 'a state of fear with no law except for the powerful', have been accused by the authorities of supporting a previously unheard-of guerrilla movement, the February 16 Resistance Army, which is alleged to operate out of Uganda. In March the information minister, Johnstone Makau, threatened to expel three foreign journalists — Joshua Hammer of *Newsweek*, Andrew Purvis of *Time* and Stephen Buckley of the *Washington Post* — who wrote articles suggesting that President Moi was trying to divert attention from internal unrest by claiming the country was threatened by foreign insurgents. (*International Herald Tribune, Independent*)

Ugandan journalists covering a football match in Kenya were arrested and threatened by police in April after President Moi blamed Ugandans for a spate of recent armed robberies. Hundreds of Ugandans, some with legal residence in Kenya, were also deported. (*New African*)

On 24 April the information minister denied reports that opposition parties had been denied broadcasting licences, and said that none had actually applied for a licence. The government, he said, is still in the process of drafting regulatory laws to govern licencing procedures. (SWB)

Recent publication: *Censorship in Kenya: Government Critics Face the Death Sentence* (A19, March 1995, 33pp)

KUWAIT

The government announced on 11 February that it will enforce a ban on civil servants

taking second jobs, a move that will seriously affect the press. Around 400 civil servants presently moonlight as journalists, often 'leaking' secret documents to their newspapers. (Reuter)

On 14 February at least 10 prisoners began a hunger strike to protest their continued detention after unfair trials before the Martial Law court in May and June 1991. They are among 24 people charged with collaborating with the Iraqi authorities, after they were forced to work on the Iraqi newspaper *al-Nida* during Iraq's occupation of Kuwait (*Index* 8/1991, 9/1991). (AI)

On 16 March the newspaper *al-Anba* was suspended for five days after it published an interview with an opposition leader who criticised government policies. (Reuter, RSF)

The authorities announced on 12 April that an Interior Ministry panel of seven members has been set up to help Parliament's Human Rights Committee investigate alleged human rights abuses. The Committee has long lobbied for greater ministerial involvement in the investigations. (Reuter)

LATVIA

Police confiscated almost 1,000 copies of a Latvian translation of *Mein Kampf* on 6 May. The books had been sent to bookshops to coincide with the 50th anniversary of the end of World War II in Europe. The book's publisher

could be charged with offences under the anti-racism laws, although President Ulmanis has reportedly expressed his support for publication of the book. (*Independent*)

LEBANON

On 11 March Johnny Mnayar, a freelance journalist, Lina Khouri of *Al Masira*, and Nawfal Daw, director of CVN television, were detained and questioned by security forces. They were accused of sympathising with militia forces. (RSF)

Joseph Njaiem, journalist with the weekly *Nahar al-Shabah*, was arrested on 25 March by security forces and held for three days, apparently in connection with an article about the presence of foreign troops in Lebanon. (RSF)

MACEDONIA

In April Fadil Sulejmani, the rector of the Albanian-language University of Tetovo, was sentenced to two-and-a-half years in prison for 'inciting resistance' in connection with the clashes between police and Albanian activists that took place when police shut the university down in February (*Index* 1&2/1995). Milaium Feizizu, a member of the university's founding committee, was sentenced to six months. (Reuter, SWB)

MALAWI

On 17 March it was reported that a theatre group could face prosecution for performing a play that refers to the murder of four politicians during the regime of Hastings Banda, on the grounds that the play could prejudice the forthcoming murder trials of Banda, his associate, John Tembo, and four police officers. (MISA)

MALAYSIA

On 30 March two journalists were arrested in Johor Baru under the Official Secrets Act for divulging 'classified information' after they quoted police sources in a report on a kidnapping case. Yusaini Ali and Saniboey Mohammed Ismail, of the daily *Harian Metro*, reported that kidnappers were demanding a US$4 million ransom. The police had asked the press not to publish stories about the case. (*Straits Times*)

MAURITIUS

Namassiwayam Ramalingum, editor of the weekly paper *L'Indépendant*, has received death threats after publishing an article on the prophet Mohammed. On 10 March large numbers of copies of the paper were burned in the streets of Port Louis and on 12 March the printing presses were firebombed. Despite repeated public incitements (including a *fatwa* issued on 17 March) by Islamists, to murder both Ramalingum and his family, the police have so far made no arrests. Publication of *L'Indépendant* has now been halted, and the editor has fled Mauritius, in fear for his life. His intended return to the country in early May had to be delayed because of a

planned demonstration by Islamists organised to meet his arrival. (*L'Indépendant*)

MEXICO

Following armed confrontations between peasants and police in Cacalomacán on 10 February, a delegation of congressional deputies visited María Gloria Guevara Niebla, Ricardo Hernández López, Hilario Martínez Hernández, Martín Trujillo Barajaz, Luis Sánchez Navarette, Alvaro Castillo Granados, Hermelinda García Zapahua, Rosa Hernández Hernández and Jorge Santiago Santiago in prison. Many of the prisoners, alleged to be members of the Zapatista National Liberation Army (EZLN), reported that they had been tortured during interrogation and forced to sign unseen confessions. (AI)

Eduardo Ibarra, editor of *Forum*, is under investigation for violating the Press Law by publishing an article entitled 'The Need for a Military Ombudsman in Mexico' by Brigadier-General José Gallardo Rodríguez. After the article appeared Gallardo Rodríguez was imprisoned in November 1994. The Mexican Commission for the Defence and Promotion of Human Rights was denied permission to visit him in prison in March. (PEN)

A Jesuit-sponsored station in Veracruz, Radio Huayacocotla, was ordered to stop broadcasting on 23 March after a technical report by the Communications and Transport Secretariat (SCT)

found minor faults in the station's antenna and equipment. The station's director has been summoned several times over the past year to answer accusations from the state government and Ministry of Justice, that it is broadcasting 'coded messages' in the region's three indigenous languages. (CCPJ)

NAMIBIA

It was reported on 17 March that pamphlets claiming that the Holocaust and the Anne Frank diaries are a hoax were distributed by Nazi sympathisers around the National Gallery in Windhoek. This report comes after the publication of a full page advertisement in the *Windhoek Advertiser*, eulogising Rudolf Hess. The Prosecutor-General is currently deciding whether or not to prosecute those responsible under Namibia's racial discrimination law. (MISA)

NIGERIA

A number of prominent Nigerian military and political figures, including former military ruler Olusegun Obasanjo and Shehu Yar'Adua, a leading member of the Constitutional Conference set up to prepare for a return to democracy, were arrested in March for allegedly plotting a coup. Obasanjo was released after 10 days but is not permitted to leave his home town. It is reported that at least 60 officers were executed following the discovery of the plot. (*Observer*, Reuter)

On 10 March State Security

TCHIK

RSF

DÉLIGNE -

Police in Lagos arrested Bayo Onanuga, director of the Independent Communication Network, the newspaper group that publishes the daily *PM News* and the weeklies the *News* and *Tempo*. No official explanation has been given for his detention, but it is thought to be linked to an article published in the *News* and *Tempo* about the coup attempt. Onanuga has since been released. (RSF, *Financial Times*)

On 15 March Chris Anyanwu, publisher and editor-in-chief of *TSM*, a Sunday magazine, was detained apparently in connection with her magazine's reporting of the alleged coup attempt. She was later released but *TSM*'s editor, Comfort Obi, has fled, fearing arrest. (PEN)

Recent publication: *Trade Unionists in Nigeria: A State of Crisis* (AI, May 1995, 4pp)

OMAN

In April the director-general of culture, Sheikh Hilal al-

Amri, opened a censor's office at the baggage counter of Seeb international airport, in order to tighten control over video cassettes brought in from abroad. (*Times, Oman*)

PAKISTAN

Factional violence continues across the country: at least seven people, including former Punjab provincial assembly member Sheikh Muhammed Iqbal, were killed in an attack on a funeral in Jhang on 5 March. A militant Sunni group, Sipah-i-Sahaba (SSP), of whom Iqbal was an opponent, was blamed for the murders. Over the Eid al-Fitr holiday period, 13 people were killed in Karachi, and at least six injured. The motives for the attacks were unknown, but at least five of the victims were connected to the Mohajir National Movement (MQM). In Lahore on 7 March Mohamad Ali Naqvi, a leader of the militant Shi'ite organisation Tehrik-i-Jafria Pakistan, was murdered. The SSP were blamed for the attack. (Reuter)

Attacks on journalists continue: armed members of Anjuman Tuliba-i-Islam ransacked and burned the offices of Ahmed Zia, the Nawabshah correspondent of *Nawa-i-Waqt*, on 10 March. In Karachi on 11 March, police beat up and detained press photographers who had gone to cover a rocket attack

on the house of Pir Syed Mardan Ali Shah, president of Pakistan Muslim League. (Pakistan Press Foundation)

Police raided the house in Nawabshah of Baksh Ali Jamali, a correspondent for *Kawish*, on 13 March. A delegation of local journalists protested the incident to the senior superintendent of police, who said it had been a 'misunderstanding'. (Pakistan Press Foundation)

Contempt of court proceedings were initiated by the government on 22 March against the editor and publisher of *Dawn* newspaper and Ardeshir Cowasajee, a regular columnist of the newspaper, charging them with having made contemptuous remarks and scandalising the judiciary in Pakistan. Two judges were nominated to inquire into possible action against papers publishing articles criticising the appointment of judges, judicial verdicts and the conduct of judges. (Pakistan Press Foundation, Pakistan Newspapers and Periodicals Association)

Iqbal Masih, a 12-year-old Christian boy, was shot dead in Muridke, near Lahore on 16 April. Iqbal was president of the children's section of the Bonded Labour Liberation Front of Pakistan (BLLFP) and had campaigned against the exploitation of child labour, particularly in the carpet weaving industry which employs over half a million child slaves. Police said Iqbal was killed by an employee of the local landlord. (Reuter)

Three people were killed in a gun battle in Hyderabad on 24 April when police arrested two Sindh provincial parliamentary deputies of the Mohajir National Movement (MQM), and sealed an office of an MQM committee. The Human Rights Commission of Pakistan (HRCP) said on 29 April that it would set up an international tribunal to investigate allegations of human rights abuses against the Mohajir community in Karachi. (Reuter)

Recent publication: *Pakistan: The Death Penalty for Juveniles*, AI, March 1995, 5pp)

PALESTINE (GAZA-JERICHO)

The ban imposed on *al-Istiqlal* newspaper (*Index* 2/1995) was lifted on 17 March but the five *al-Istiqlal* journalists arrested — Atiyeh Abu Mansour, Khaled Sadeq, Nahed Kutkut, Muhammed Sayyad and Zakariya Madhun — are still being held without charge. Alaa al-Saftawi, *al-Istiqlal*'s publisher also arrested on 6 February, was released on 2 March. (AI, Reuter)

Raji Sourani (*Index* 2/1995), director of the Gaza Centre for Rights and Law, was dismissed by the Centre's board on 1 April and the organisation's offices were closed. Following protests by staff against his firing, they too were dismissed. According to a statement by Sourani, the dismissals came after the Centre protested against the Palestinian Authority's new security courts (see p12).

(*Jerusalem Times*)

Taher al-Nounou, Gaza correspondent for the East Jerusalem-based newspaper *An-Nahar*, was arrested by Palestinian police on 5 April after he wrote an article disputing the official explanation of the 2 April explosion in Gaza, which killed six suspected Hamas militants. (*Jerusalem Times*, RSF)

The PNA crackdown on suspected Islamic groups following the 9 April car bombings in Gaza resulted in the arrests of over 300 people, including several journalists. On 9 April Alaa al-Masharawy, reporter with *al-Quds*, was arrested at Erez checkpoint, and Muhammed Jahjouh, a freelance cameraman, was arrested at his home in Shati refugee camp. On 10 April Amer Shriteh, CBS News stringer, was arrested while filming a protest by Islamic Jihad activists. On 13 April police raided the home of Taher Shriteh, publisher of *Filastin* magazine and stringer for Reuter and CBS News. Taher was not at home but police assaulted his brothers Fakher, Amer and Zaher. Also on 13 April Ghazi Hamad, deputy editor at *al-Watan*, was assaulted by police during a raid on the paper's Gaza offices. He and two other *al-Watan* journalists, editor-in-chief Sayed Abu Musameh and reporter Nafez al-Ji'b, were arrested and detained for several hours. The raid came after *al-Watan* compared the Palestinian Authority's crackdown with the Israeli occupation. (CPJ, RSF)

Imad al-Faluji, editor of *al-Watan*, was questioned by police on 29 April over an article in the paper alleging that Hamas leader Nidal Dabbus is being held by PNA security forces, a charge they deny. (SWB)

PARAGUAY

Hugo Cano Gimenez, reporter for the daily *ABC Color* in the city of Ayolas, was beaten by an airforce officer and had his camera destroyed on 6 March, while covering a military air crash. (Paraguayan Journalists' Union)

PERU

On 14 February Augusto Ernesto LLosa Giraldo, editor of the newspaper *El Casmeno* and reporter for *Radio Casma*, was arrested in Casma. The charges relate to a terrorist case going back to 1986, when he was asked to testify as a witness but failed to appear and was found in contempt of court. While arresting the journalist, the police confiscated documents including posters of the National Association of Journalists, and a recent issue of their magazine *La Pluma*. (FIP)

Anonymous tribunals, set up to hear cases of terrorism, are to be eliminated on 15 October. When the law comes into effect, those held on terrorist charges will have the right to request legal representation from the moment of arrest, those under the age of 18 will no longer be subject to jail sentences, and the cases will come directly to magistrates designated by the Executive Council of the Judiciary and the Supreme Public Prosecutor's Committee. (Instituto Prensa y Sociedad)

PHILIPPINES

The film *Sibak* (Midnight Dancers), the first Filipino film to draw worldwide acclaim, was banned in April. Legal technicalities in licencing the film for screening and export had not been observed, although these are rarely enforced. The chairman of the Movie and Television Review and Classification Board said the film was 'immoral, indecent, and exploitative' due to its homosexual protagonists and subject matter. (*Philippine Daily Inquirer*)

POLAND

The Sejm amended the broadcasting law on 17 March to allow the National Radio and TV Broadcasting Council to elect its own chair, rather than having to accept a presidential appointee. (SWB)

On 30 March the Interior Ministry announced that many more files from the Communist secret police archive would be made available to historians. Journalists seeking access to the archive will still have to apply directly to the interior minister for permission. (SWB)

ROMANIA

The mayor of Cluj, Gheorghe Funar, banned all public meetings on 15 March,

including an ethnic-Hungarian rally to mark Hungary's national day. Funar said Romanian nationalist groups had also applied to hold rallies that day. Some 300 ethnic Hungarians defied the ban. (OMRI)

On 6 April Radio and Television Free Trade Union leader Dumitru Iuga ended his 36-day hunger strike in protest at alleged political interference in the state media, after the nomination of Paul Soloc to the Radio and Television Council was withdrawn. The dispute arose when Parliament substituted Soloc's candidature for that of Gabriel Liiceanu, one of two candidates for the Council elected by state television employees. On 28 April, employees confirmed their choice of Liiceanu. (OMRI)

On 26 April 24 journalists from the daily *Tineretul Liber*, including editor-in-chief Monica Zvirjinschi, resigned complaining of editorial interference by the paper's publishers. The paper has announced a suspension of publication pending reorganisation. (OMRI)

The government has changed the official name for Roma to 'Tigani', it was reported on 2 May. Roma leaders object to the change saying that 'Tigani' is a direct translation of 'gypsy' and is often used pejoratively. (OMRI)

RUSSIAN FEDERATION

Russia: The Moscow Prosecutor's Office brought a

case against the writer and journalist Yaroslav Mogutin (*Index* 1/1995, p66) on 30 March for 'inflaming national, social and religious division' in an article he wrote for *Novyi Vzglyad* about the war in Chechnya. The charge carries a maximum seven-year prison sentence. The Presidential Commission on Information and Press Subjects has also recommended that the press minister rescind *Novyi Vzglyad*'s publishing licence. (PEN)

The controversial privatisation of the state broadcasting company, Ostankino, came under attack in early April from the State Duma, which voted to suspend the creation of the new Russian Public TV (ORT) until the relevant federal law is passed. (SWB)

Yevgeny Nikitin, a journalist with ITAR-TASS news agency, was beaten near a Moscow metro station on 17 April. Several documents were stolen in the attack, the eighth on journalists from the agency in the past six months. (SWB)

It was reported on 21 April that lawsuits had been brought against the radio station Mayak and 2x2, a television station, both of which had sold airtime to the Japanese religious cult Aum Shinrikyo, which carried out a gas attack on the Tokyo metro in March. The same day Vice-Premier Sergei Shakhray announced that a new law to limit the activities of foreign missionaries is currently in preparation. (Ekho Moskvy, SWB)

On 26 April the official newspaper *Rossiskaya Gazeta* criticised a draft presidential decree which, it said, would create a 'censorship committee' headed by State Press Committee Chairman Sergei Gryzunov. Also on 26 April, at a meeting with news agency heads, the first deputy prime minister called for unbiased coverage of Chechnya. Information provided by the Russian government was going unused, he said, while 'pro-Dudayev propaganda' is widely circulated. (OMRI, SWB)

Steve Levine, a US journalist whose articles on the war in Chechnya included accounts of alleged atrocities committed by Russian troops, was detained on arrival at Moscow's Vnukova airport in late April, declared an 'undesirable person' and barred from entering the country. The Foreign Ministry later explained that under a 1992 agreement between CIS members, Russia cannot admit foreign citizens who have been refused entry to another member state. Levine was expelled from Uzbekistan in September 1994 because of his unfavourable reporting of President Karimov (*Index* 6/1994). (*Moscow Times*)

Alexander Nikonov and Dmitry Bykov, journalists with the weekly *Sobesednik*, were released from custody pending trial for 'vicious hooliganism' in late April. The charges arose from an article, published on April Fool's Day, entitled 'Mat' (Russian for offensive language) which contained obscene words. *Sobesednik*'s editor, Andrei Dyatlov, claims the charges are in retaliation for recent articles exposing corruption in the State Duma. (*Moscow Times*)

Chechnya: Human rights monitors, including a deputation of Duma members, reported on 11 April that they had been prevented from entering the village of Samashki to check allegations of gross human rights violations there. The Russian Interior Ministry denied the reports, saying that only one part of the village, which was still resisting Russian forces, was closed to outsiders. The following day, the Duma members were granted permission to visit the village, but their armed escort allegedly took them not to Samashki, but to Asinovskaya station. (SWB)

RWANDA

The government, concerned at unfavourable international publicity, blocked access to satellite dishes used by foreign news networks for transmitting images abroad in late April. (*International Herald Tribune*)

André Sibomana (*Index* 3/1994, 1/1995), editor of *Kinyamateka* newspaper, was reported in early May to have been receiving death threats from the head of intelligence for the Rwandan Patriotic Front in Gitarama region. Sibomana subsequently went into hiding for three days, after also being threatened with arrest. (CCPJ)

SERBIA-MONTENEGRO

Kosovo: On 7 March police forcibly closed the Xheladin Deda medical high school in Mitrovica. On 10 March police reportedly arrested Muharrem Merovci, a teacher at a Vushtrii technical school and three other teachers at a Vushtrii elementary school, both Albanian-language schools. (SWB)

It was reported in March that at least 20 Albanian men have been arrested on charges of desertion after Serbian authorities sent out draft notices for the Yugoslav army to ethnic Albanians. (OMRI)

In Gnjilane in April six ethnic Albanians were detained for 'associating in order to carry out hostile activity'. Of the 159 former policemen arrested since November 1994, 16 have so far been sentenced on charges relating to the setting up of a 'shadow interior ministry and security service' and 'endangering the integrity of Yugoslavia'. (OMRI, Reuter)

Recent publications: *Kosovo Albanians II* (Humanitarian Law Centre, Belgrade, Spotlight Report no 16, February 1995, 31pp); *The Trial of General Trifunovic* (Humanitarian Law Centre, Belgrade Spotlight Report no 17, March 1995, 7pp)

SIERRA LEONE

On 13 March Rowland Martyn, a journalist with the weekly *Week End Spark*, was arrested by police from the Central Investigation

Department and questioned about a photograph that appeared in the 10 March edition of the paper, showing a Sierra Leone army captain who had defected to the Revolutionary United Front (RUF). Rowland was released 10 days later. (RSF)

On 13 April Siaka Massaquoi, president of the Sierra Leone Association of Journalists (SLAJ) and editor of *Independent Vision*, and Max Corneh, a journalist on the paper, were detained in connection with a front-page story in the paper entitled 'Police Beg Driver to Board Taxi as Rebels Advance'. The story told how government soldiers in a town under attack by the RUF begged a taxi driver to help them flee the fighting. (*Gambian Daily Observer*, Reuter)

SLOVAKIA

On 2 March the daily papers *Pravda, Narodna Obroda, Praca, Novy Cas, Smena, Sme* and *Uj Szo* criticised government plans to increase taxes on publishers and broadcasters whose companies are more than 30 per cent foreign owned. On 6 March several of the dailies printed a blank page with a warning about the tax. (IFJ, OMRI)

Some 7,000 people attended a march in Bratislava on 9 March, organised by the Christian Democratic Movement (KDH) to protest government attacks on free speech and demand the reinstatement of the popular television satires, *Apropo, Halusky*

and *The Milan Marcovic Evening Show* (*Index* 2/1995). (OMRI)

The ruling Movement for a Democratic Slovakia (HZDS) announced that all government information would be channelled through an official spokesman from 18 March, and that the party's Press and Information Department would be replaced by a Public Relations Department. The announcement came in the wake of severe criticism by the prime minister, Vladimir Meciar, of the way journalists report official statements. On 25 March reporters complained that they were excluded from covering the proceedings of the HZDS party congress. (SWB)

SOUTH AFRICA

The Advertising Standards Authority has come into conflict with the Cellphone Service provider, MTN, after banning an MTN advertisement with the slogan 'better connection'. The ban, initially upheld because of a prohibition on comparative advertising, may not stand up to a constitutional court test on freedom of expression. John Farqhar, editor of *AdVantage* trade magazine, speaking in defence of the ban, said: 'We have a largely illiterate and native population here. If we were to let loose advertising hyperbole on them it could be damaging.' (*Weekly Mail & Guardian*)

Draft legislation made public on 2 March will exempt theatrical productions, and art

and literature from censorship controls. The concept of blasphemy is also to be abolished. The draft document criticises the existing censorship system as undemocratic, unconstitutional and intrusive upon the freedom of adults. (*Guardian*)

Officials unsuccessfully attempted to confiscate transmitters belonging to the unlicenced, extreme right-wing station Radio Donkerhoek on 26 April. Police say they will continue to monitor the station's broadcasts. (SWB)

SOUTH KOREA

On 11 and 12 March Ki Seh-Moon and Lee Kyung Ryol were arrested under the National Security Law, apparently for printing a pamphlet about Yoon Ki-Nam, a captured North Korean soldier, which was intended for distribution at his funeral. (AI)

On 21 March Kim Mu-Yong, a history lecturer at Bangsong Tongshin University, was arrested for possessing, distributing, and producing writings on the Korean guerrilla movement 1948-53. Under Korean law, nothing may be written that 'praises, benefits or encourages' North Korea. (PEN)

Writer and activist Hwang Suk-Young (*Index* 5&6/1993, 10/1993) began his third year in prison under the National Security Law on 27 April. (PEN)

SRI LANKA

Sinha Ratunga, editor of the *Sunday Times*, was formally

charged on 29 March with criminally defaming president Kumaratunga (*Index* 2/1995). (Reuter)

Recent publications: *Censorship and Media Reform in Sri Lanka*, (A19, March 1995, 22pp); *Time for Truth and Justice: Observations and Recommendations Regarding the Commissions Investigating Past Human Rights Violations* (AI, April 1995, 25pp)

SUDAN

In Khartoum in late February security forces forcibly broke up a demonstration by the relatives of 28 army officers who were executed in 1990. Several demonstrators were beaten and threatened with rape, and one, Kamal Abualgasim, was seized by the police and has disappeared. It is thought he is being held in one of the notorious 'ghost houses' in which suspected opponents are tortured and held indefinitely. (AI)

SWAZILAND

Four journalists with the *Swazi Observer* were imprisoned on 3 March on the instruction of the director for public prosecutions. No explanation has been given why the four were arrested, or whether they will be charged. The arrests took place hours after the information and broadcasting minister and the minister of finance were dismissed from the government for their part in illicit car deals. The *Swazi Observer* carried several stories about the dismissals. (MISA)

TAJIKISTAN

On 1 May Mirzo Salimov, correspondent for the Moscow-based Tajik opposition paper Charogi Ruz, was arrested by people dressed in military uniform who told him: 'You are the enemy of the people. We have been looking for you for a long time.' The police, and the Internal and Security Ministries all deny that they are holding Salimov, and his current whereabouts remain unknown. (CPJ)

TANZANIA

Eleven media workers are facing criminal charges as the government increases pressure on the independent media before elections in October. Sam Makla, editor of the Kiswahili daily, *Majira*, and its publishers, Rashidi Mbuguni and Richard Nyaulawa, are charged with sedition and withholding information over government plans to buy radar equipment. A freelance journalist, Edina Ndejembi, has been charged with 'insulting a police officer on duty' while covering an opposition rally in Moshi in March, which was broken up by police. Four journalists and three print shop workers of the magazine *Mwana-Mama* and *Heko* remain on trial for publishing pornography following an exposé of the porn industry in *Mwana-Mama* (*Index* 2/1995). (MISA)

THAILAND

On 26 April the Bangkok Criminal Court dismissed a *lèse majesté* case against writer Sulak Sivaraksa (*Index* 3/1993), who was charged with insulting the monarchy and defaming General Suchinda Krapraoon, commander-in-chief of the armed forces. Sivaraksa has been on trial since June 1993. (PEN)

TIBET

A three-page document obtained by the Tibetan government in exile gives the first indication of force being used to implement China's birth-control policy. The document, issued in 1991, is a set of county-level regulations for Chabcha, in the Tibetan area of Amdo, calling for the imposition of 'birth prevention operations', without delay and without appeal, on those who exceed the prescribed number of children. (Tibet Information Network)

Gyalten Kelsang, a nun imprisoned for two years for her part in a pro-independence demonstration in 1993, died on 20 February, apparently as a result of maltreatment and poor living conditions in prison. (Tibet Information Network)

A total of 16 pro-independence demonstrations were reported in February and March, with 106 monks and nuns being arrested in Lhasa and Phenpo, mostly from the Nalanda monastery, according to unofficial sources. A report in the official *Tibet Daily* in early March reiterated the authorities' commitment to imposing limits on the number of monks in each monastery, and ordered all monks to 'politically draw a clear line of demarcation between themselves and the Dalai clique'. (Tibet Information Network)

On 5 April the official Tibet People's Broadcasting Station reported that authorities have seized tens of thousands of 'reactionary propaganda materials' in Tibet since the beginning of the year. (SWB)

TUNISIA

Moncef Marzouki (*Index* 3/1994, 6/1994), a medical professor and human rights activist, has twice been prevented from leaving the country recently: in March his passport was confiscated by security officials at the airport as he was on his way to a medical conference in Brussels; and on 22 April he was prevented from attending the Arab Organisation for Human Rights annual meeting in Cairo. (AAASHRAN)

TURKEY

According to statistics issued by the Ministry of Justice, a total of 1,774 trials were held at the Istanbul State Security Court in 1994, 65 per cent of them concerning press offences, with 2,098 journalists and editors being prosecuted. At the end of 1994 at least 74 Turkish reporters and editors were in jail for 'separatist' offences. (*Kurdistan News*, CPJ)

New discipline regulations in secondary education, introduced on 31 January, allow the Disciplinary Council to subject female students to virginity tests, with powers to expel those who fail them. (*Info-Turk*)

Five private television channels — Kanal 21, Metro, Can, Mega and Yildiz — and 16 private radio stations — Degisim, Ses, Metro, Kent, Show, Bag, Nur, Mega, Diyar, Can, Malabadi, Genc, Super, FM, Klas and Star — in Diyarbakir were banned at the end of January on the grounds that they interfered with police and military wireless transmission and were detrimental to broadcasting by the state broadcaster TRT. The owners of the stations claim that their transmitters meet legal requirements and that different standards are being applied to different regions in Turkey. (*Kurdistan News*)

From 27 March foreign correspondents and Turkish journalists working for foreign media were prevented by the military from entering northern Iraq. Murat Ersavci, Turkey's director of press and information, said the restrictions had been imposed 'for safety reasons'. On 29 March Ersavci announced that limited access would be granted to journalists, but only if they were accompanied by the Turkish military. (CPJ)

The offices of a new pro-Kurdish newspaper, *Yeni Politika*, were raided in the second week of April, before it had published its first issue. Six journalists were detained for three days and the inau-gural issue was confiscated for containing separatist propaganda. (CPJ)

Necmiye Arslanoglu, a journalist formerly with the banned daily *Özgür Gündem*, was arrested in a raid on a Kurdish magazine in Diyarbakir on 12 April, and is apparently being held in the Central Closed Prison there. (Kurdistan Information Centre)

Recent publication: *The Law: Freedom of Expression and Human Rights Advocacy in Turkey* (Bar Human Rights Committee, Kurdistan Human Rights Project and the Law Society, March 1995, 14pp plus appendices)

UGANDA

Following the liberalisation of Ugandan radio, two new television stations have now been given licences. Cablesat and Stem Cable are expected to provide a strong challenge to the state-run Ugandan Television. (Africom)

The editor of the *Citizen*, Lawrence Kiwanuka, was arrested on 14 April and has been charged with sedition over an article examining internal turmoil in the intelligence service (ESO) and participation of the regular army (NRA) in fighting between the Rwandan Patriotic Front and the forces of the former Rwandan Government. (RSF)

UKRAINE

Vladimir Ivanov, editor-in-chief of the daily paper *Slava*

Sevastopolya, died on 18 April of injuries sustained in a remote-controlled bomb attack four days previously. Ivanov was an ethnic Russian and his paper supported greater autonomy for the predominantly Russian population of the Crimea. Observers believe his murder is linked to his reports on organised crime and official corruption. (CPJ, SWB)

UNITED KINGDOM

On 3 March police confirmed that Britain's first prosecution over the alleged use of the internet for distribution of pornography would be brought in April. The 1994 Criminal Justice Act widened the definition of publication in the Obscene Publications Act to include computer transmission. (*The Lawyer*)

The civil servant in charge of open government, Andrew Whetnall, said on 15 March that the government was deliberately trying to keep down the number of requests from the public for official information because of the difficulties of coping with a large number of questions. He said that the open government code, which came into force in April 1994, is being underused because people are not aware of their new rights. (Campaign for Freedom of Information)

On 23 March the Cabinet agreed an outline for a new Bill to crack down on asylum seekers and illegal immigrants by tightening visa requirements for all entrants to the

country. It seems likely that the regulations will be extended to cover some Commonwealth countries for the first time. (*Times*)

The BBC lost a court battle with the main opposition parties in Scotland over permission to transmit an interview with Prime Minister John Major north of the border on 4 April. The court ruled that the interview might influence the outcome of the local government elections two days later. (*Financial Times*)

On 13 April it was announced that Quentin Tarantino's film *Reservoir Dogs* will be released uncut on video after the British Board of Film Classification ended its two-year ban. (*Guardian*)

Ragbir Singh, editor of a Punjab-language newspaper based in Smethwick near Birmingham, was imprisoned without trial in late April as 'a threat to national security'. He now faces deportation, although he has lived in Britain for 15 years without being convicted of any offence. (National Union of Journalists)

On 2 May the Independent Television Commission asked British television companies to stop showing an advertisement, for the group Survival International, on the plight of tribal peoples around the world, on the grounds that Survival International is a 'political' organisation and therefore barred from television advertising. (Survival International)

USA

On 6 January, 10 years after Bullfrog Films of Pennsylvania sued the US Information Agency, the government agreed to award educational certificates to five independent documentary films. The certificates entitle them to tax-free export status. In 1985, the USIA labelled the films 'propaganda', in effect making their international distribution impossible (*Index* 7/1988). (*Washington Post*)

The American Library Association's Office for Intellectual Freedom recorded 760 challenges to books in 1994, an increase of 8.3 per cent over the year before. The most challenged book was *Daddy's Roommate*, a picture book about a gay family, by Michael Wilhoite. The most challenged author was Alvin Schwartz. (ALA *Newsletter on Intellectual Freedom*)

The Communications Decency Act of 1995 was unanimously approved by the Senate Commerce Committee on 23 March. The measure was altered to make electronic bulletin board providers responsible only for 'knowingly transmitting communication that is obscene, lewd, lascivious, filthy or indecent'. It was incorporated into the omnibus Telecommunications Bill that will be debated by the full Senate this spring. (People for the American Way, *Boston Globe*)

On 30 March a federal judge in New York ruled that the military's 'don't ask, don't tell'

'And to think that in the USA they have a superhighway for information!'

The order reverses a system of intense classification that has been in place for the past decade (*Index* 1&2/ 1994). (Associated Press)

In the aftermath of the bombing of a federal office building in Oklahoma City on 19 April, radio stations pulled right-wing talk shows from the air. *The Intelligence Report,* hosted by Mark Koernke, who may have connections to a suspect in the bombing, was suspended indefinitely by World Wide Christian Radio, a shortwave station in Nashville, Tennessee. A station in Michigan pulled James (Bo) Gritz off the air, but resumed broadcasting after listeners complained. When G Gordon Liddy advised listeners about how to shoot federal agents, stations in Connecticut and Ohio suspended his programme, and the Oklahoma Senate voted unanimously to urge broadcasters and sponsors to stop funding the show. In a speech in Minneapolis on 24 April, President Clinton appeared to condemn extremist talk show hosts, though he did not name them directly. (Associated Press, *New York Times, Boston Globe*)

Also in response to the bombing, the President and Congress proposed strict measures to combat domestic terrorism, including increased involvement of the FBI and

policy for gay service members violates their rights to free speech and equal protection under the law. The lawsuit was brought by six people who objected to the policy (*Index* 3/1994). The judge ordered the Defense Department to stop enforcing the policy against the six, but the effect of the ruling is expected to be much broader. (national press)

In April, the government announced plans to institute new rules which will force military personnel, government employees and contractors with access to classified information to agree to allow the government to investigate their financial dealings as a condition of employment. The policy is a response to the 1994 Aldrich Ames spy scandal, which involved payment

for spying. (*Washington Post*)

On 4 April a federal appeals court in New York reversed itself and decided that the First Amendment rights of Leonard Jeffries, a professor of black studies at City College of New York, were not violated when he was removed as chairman of that department in 1992 after making an anti-Semitic speech. The Supreme Court had ordered the lower court to reconsider its first ruling in light of a recent Supreme Court decision (*Index* 7/1993). (Associated Press, ALA *Newsletter on Intellectual Freedom*)

On 17 April President Clinton signed an executive order requiring that all top secret, secret and confidential documents 25 years or older be automatically declassified.

the military in criminal investigations, greater access to financial and travel records of alleged terrorists, lesser requirements for wiretapping authorisation, and the criminalising of financial support to organisations deemed by the President to be terrorist. After civil libertarians objected, the government said on 3 May that it would not seek absolute power for the President in designating terrorist groups. Other aspects of the proposed legislation remained in place. (Associated Press, *Boston Globe*)

A Supreme Court ruling on 19 April affirmed the right to distribute anonymous political pamphlets as 'the essence of First Amendment expression'. The case involved Margaret McIntyre of Columbus, Ohio, who, in 1988, was fined for handing out unsigned leaflets opposing a proposed school tax. The ruling overturns laws in all states, except California, which ban political flyers that do not identify the sponsor. (Associated Press)

Recent publications: *Artistic Freedom Under Attack*, Volume 3 (People for the American Way, 1995); *Current Voices — An Expert Rolodex: a Resource for Media Professionals* (Institute for Alternative Journalism, San Francisco, 1995); *United States: A World Leader in Executing Juveniles* (HRW/Children's Rights Project, March 1995, 22pp); *Crossing the Line: Human Rights Abuses Along the US Border with Mexico Persist* (HRW/Americas, April 1995, 37pp)

UZBEKISTAN

Several activists with the banned party Erk (Freedom) were found guilty of plotting a coup and of charges relating to the production of the party's newspaper on 31 March (*Index* 4&5/1994). Muhammed Solih and Murad Dzhurayev each received 12 years, Erkin Asurov 10 years, and the party's press secretary, Diloprom Iskhakova, 6 years suspended. (SWB)

VANUATU

The finance minister threatened to revoke the licence of the country's only independent paper, *Trading Post*, on 5 April after it criticised the granting of a trading licence to a Taiwanese bank. The paper's publisher said that if the threats continue, he will have to stop reporting local stories. (SWB)

YEMEN

On 5 April Hussein Muhammad Nasser, editor-in-chief of the now-defunct weekly *al-Jadid*, Fadl Ali Mubarak, Abin correspondent for the Aden-based daily *14th of October*, and Ali Abdullah Munser, Abin correspondent for the SABA news agency, were reportedly arrested by political security officers in a round-up of members of the Yemeni Socialist Party in the Abin region. (CPJ)

ZAMBIA

Chief Justice Matthew Ngulube awarded K1million (US$1,500) in libel damages to health minister Michael Sata against the bi-weekly *Post* newspaper in late February, in connection with articles attacking Sata's fitness to be a minister. The paper, which has received more than 100 legal writs since launching in 1991, hailed the decision as a victory for press freedom, however, citing the relatively small damages award. The court also refused Sata's request for a permanent injunction against the paper reporting on him in future. Sata has appealed against the ruling, and the *Post* has since lodged a counter-appeal. (MISA)

On 22 April George Malunga, editor of the weekly *Crime News*, was questioned by police and accused of 'being in possession of pornography'. The 17 April edition of *Crime News* had reproduced, with pictures, a number of articles debating issues relating to nudity and pornography from MISA's publication *Free Press*. (MISA) ❑

***

Compiled by: Anna Feldman, Jason Garner, Oren Gruenbaum (Africa); Nathalie de Brogio, Nan Levinson, Nathalie Vartanpour-Naalbandian (Americas); Nicholas McAulay, Atanu Roy, Jason Stephens (Asia); Colin Isham (central Asia); Laura Bruni, Robin Jones, Vera Rich (eastern Europe and CIS); Jamie McLeish, Philippa Nugent (Middle East); Daniel Brett, Robert Maharajh (western Europe) ❑

Contributors

Yuri Afanasev is Rector of the Russian State University for the Humanities; **Alexander Bely** graduated from the Belarusian Polytechnic Academy in 1989; **Guy Berger** is a Professor at the Department of Journalism and Media Studies at Rhodes University and ex-editor of *South* newspaper in Cape Town; **Yelena Bonner** married Andrei Sakharov in 1972 and now works with the Sakharov Foundation; **Achmat Dangor** grew up in the townships near Johannesburg and now works as a rural development specialist. His latest novel, *Rasputin's in the Garden* (from which Mama & Kid Freedom is taken), will be published in South Africa towards the end of 1995; **Ronald Dworkin** is Professor of Jurisprudence at the University of Oxford; **Felipe Fernández-Armesto**'s *Millennium: a History of Our Last Thousand Years* will be published by Transworld in September, 1995; **Robert Fisk** is the Middle East correspondent for the London *Independent*; **Eduardo Galeano** is Uruguay's leading writer. Foremost among his books are *Memory of Fire, Open Veins of Latin America, Days and Nights of Love and War* and *The Book of Embraces;* **Altaf Gauhar** is a leading columnist in Urdu- and English-language newspapers in Pakistan; **Nadine Gordimer** lives in Johannesburg. She was awarded the Nobel Prize for Literature in 1991. Her latest novel, *None to Accompany Me,* was published last year and a collection of essays, *Writing and Being,* will be published by Harvard University Press in September; novelist **Christopher Hope** was born in Johannesburg and now lives in London. His most recent work is *The Love Songs of Nathan J Swirsky*; **Rhys Johnson** was legal officer to the Gaza Centre for Rights and Law. He and Raji Sourani are establishing a new human rights organisation in Gaza; **Harvey J Kaye** is the Ben & Joyce Rosenberg Professor of Social Change and Development and Director of the Center for History and Social Change at the University of Wisconsin-Green Bay. His *The Education of Desire: Marxists and the Writing of History* (Routledge) was awarded the 1993 Isaac Deutscher Memorial Prize; **Baruch Kimmerling** is Professor of Sociology at the Hebrew University of Jerusalem; **Lara Marlowe** is the Beirut Bureau Chief for *TIME Magazine*; **Caroline Moorehead** is a writer and film maker specialising in human rights; **Nicole Pope** is *Le Monde*'s correspondent in Turkey; **Ihnat Sahanovic** is lecturer in history in the Institute of History at the Belarus Academy of Sciences and founding editor of the *Belarusian Historical Review*; **Jeremy Scott** is a freelance writer on Japan and is currently translating a book on Japanese politics; **Robert Service** is Professor of Russian History and Politics at the London School of Slavonic and East European Studies. The third volume of his trilogy, *Lenin: A Political Life,* was published this year; **Peter Sullivan** is editor of *The Star* and **Gabu Tugwana** of *New Nation,* both in Johannesburg; **Darrin Wood** is co-author of the documentary *Chiapas: Testimony of the Ejido Morelia* and writes on international affairs for the Basque newspaper *EGIN;* **Jeff Zerbst** is associate editor of South Africa's *Hustler* magazine. ❑